Variability

Not Disability

Struggling Readers in a Workshop Classroom

Cathy M. Roller
University of Iowa
Iowa City, Iowa

INTERNATIONAL
**Reading
Association**
800 Barksdale Road, PO Box 8139
Newark, Delaware 19714-8139, USA

The International Reading Association attempts, through its publications, to provide a forum for a wide spectrum of opinions on reading. This policy permits divergent viewpoints without implying the endorsement of the Association.

Director of Publications   Joan M. Irwin
Assistant Director of Publications   Wendy Lapham Russ
Associate Editor   Christian A. Kempers
Associate Editor   Matthew W. Baker
Assistant Editor   Janet Parrack
Production Department Manager   Iona Sauscermen
Graphic Design Coordinator   Boni Nash
Design Consultant   Larry Husfelt
Desktop Publishing Supervisor   Wendy Mazur
Desktop Publisher   Anette Schütz-Ruff
Desktop Publisher   Cheryl Strum
Production Services Editor   David Roberts

Library of Congress Cataloging in Publication Data
    Roller, Cathy M.
    Variability not disability: struggling readers in a workshop classroom/Cathy M. Roller.
        p.   cm.
    Includes bibliographical references and index.
    1. Learning disabled children—Education (Elementary)—Iowa—Reading—Case studies.
2. Reading—Remedial teaching—Iowa—Case studies.   I. Title.
LC4704.87.R65   1996   95-46674
371.91'44—dc20
ISBN 0-87207-142-1 (pbk.)

Contents

Foreword

VARIABILITY NOT *Disability: Struggling Readers in a Workshop Classroom* is about enabling reading growth and ability, the ultimate goal of reading diagnosis, reading clinics, and all reading teachers. Numerous books detail how to identify disabled readers, choose and interpret tests, select instruction and materials, write reports, and so forth, yet few of them mark out a practical, day-to-day instructional framework for working with struggling readers. Here is one that does just that. In your hands is a most sensible and clear guide to helping these readers become independent. As one reading teacher to another, this book is a find and a boon.

Historically, the focus of remediation has been one of separating out and starting over. A reading specialist's job is seen as searching out children who fail and re-instructing—repeating particularly those easily identified bits and pieces of reading, the "skills." Remedial clinics also habitually lag behind any changes made in the rest of reading practice. The majority of our reading fellowship may progress in thought and action, but remedial instruction remains static. With some wonderful exceptions, reading clinics are the most conservative element in the reading community. Curiously, in being so, conservative clinics rely on exactly what research says not to: focus on behavior, rules, and rote repetition. The attitudes, interests, and personal learning timeframes of struggling readers are not taken into consideration, nor are their surrounding family influences. Readers' understanding of their own process and progress is ignored. And the children, the struggling readers for whom good instruction can make the most difference, become less able. Rather than accepting this deficit model we are so accustomed to, Roller provides us with a fresh way of thinking. Her approach to remedial instruction focuses on seeking out, reinforcing, and building on the capability of struggling readers. She asks us to look for what they *can* do instead of what they can't.

At the same time that we depend on an insufficient model to instruct struggling readers, the economic reality is that more children are being labeled as special learners and less money for separate instruction from specialized teachers is available. The diagnosis and instruction of struggling readers is now being left on the insufficiently prepared shoulders of classroom teachers. In her book, Roller adapts the reading and writing workshop approach practiced in many classrooms and makes it usable for any teacher of struggling readers, whether in clinic or classroom.

Written from the insights of her own clinic experiences and the conviction that struggling readers are like all other readers, Roller convinces us that, given the appropriate context, struggling readers are just as capable of seeking the knowledge and making the connections needed to solve the puzzle of reading as their more proficient classmates. Based on a teaching approach that honors children's ability, competence, and intellect, this method frees them to become self-motivating, self-directing, and thus, independent readers. It recognizes that struggling readers are not "dis"-anything, that they are as able as any other. It challenges each one of us to make the conceptualization of our classrooms and clinics more genuine and our instruction more realistic.

Mary Dayton Sakari
University of Victoria, British Columbia

Acknowledgments

I **WOULD** like to thank the children who participate in the University of Iowa Speech, Hearing, & Reading Clinic's Summer Residential Program (SRP), on which this book is based, and their families. The children have taught me much over the years, and the work I do at the University is always tempered by the reality of the SRP children. I hope in writing this book I have put the lessons learned from them to good use.

I also thank my colleagues at Wendell Johnson Speech and Hearing Clinic. I mention three by name because over the years they have taken care of the nuts and bolts of SRP—Robert Schum, Penelope Hall, and Kathy Miller. Penny has served in many roles at SRP including most recently as director. In every role she has been supportive. Kathy has kept track of the details and persisted with reminders until I came through. Bob, as the director and staff psychologist, has performed many roles, not the least of which is a supporter through some difficult moments. I am indebted, too, to all the graduate and undergraduate students who have worked with me in various capacities. I couldn't possibly mention them all, but as they know, it took the dedication of every one of them to make SRP happen.

I also thank the University of Iowa for its continuing support. SRP will celebrate its 50th anniversary this summer, and it has had critical institutional support through all those years. Also I must thank the University for supporting my research program in various ways. The FINE Foundation of Iowa funded the transcription of many of the examples in the book as parts of research grants; the transcription has been essential to my learning over the years.

I thank the faculty, students, and former students who are or have been members of the Literacy Research Group at the University of Iowa. Linda Fielding, Penny Beed, and Sylvia Forsyth are listed on specific chapters because we have pursued the work together. I have cited Jim Marshall, Peg Finders, Cynthia Lewis, Norma Linda Gonzalez, Marilyn Ohlhausen, Mike Ford, and Mary Jepsen because some of their work touches directly on this work. And I have mentioned Jan Schmitt-Craven, Charlene Hall, and Theresa Kearney because they were actors in some of the scenes I depict. Marilyn Ohlhausen, Penny Beed, Linda Fielding, Joyce Hood Boettcher, Sylvia Forsyth, Gayle Bray, Jeanne Janson, Jean Hammons, Carolyn Colvin, Kathy Whitmore, Bonnie Sunstein, Cynthia Lewis, Deb Pittman, and Laurie Leutscher have read various drafts and given me feedback over the years.

I also thank the University of Iowa Division of Curriculum and Instruction support staff—Peggy Shannon, Gloria Lawrence, Erma Sattler, Beth McCabe, Sandie Hughes, and Val Dentino—mostly because they are always there for me. The week of the final deadline, as always something unexpected happened, and they pitched in to finish the details so that the manuscript would reach IRA on time. I thank Beth specifically for the work she did on the figures.

I also thank Joan Irwin and the IRA Publications Division for supporting this project. I especially thank my editor Christian Kempers for her careful, sensible work which improved the manuscript.

Some people's influence on this project has been less direct but critical nonetheless because each has contributed to my professional development. Joyce Hood Boettcher is foremost among these. She is the brightest, most perceptive scholar, teacher, and teacher of reading teachers I have ever known. I consider having worked with her to be one of the true privileges of my life. Thanks also to Betty Forell who supervised me as I supervised my first practicum students in the University of Iowa Children's Reading Clinic. Betty taught me to be a supervisor. Jeanetta Kirkpatrick and Martha Kinney also helped me survive my first SRP. My retired colleagues Jack Bagford, John Conner, and Louise Beltramo, and Beatrice Furner (who is about to join them) are still around occasionally to provide that extra boost.

Also important to my professional development have been the Language Arts Resource Specialists of the Iowa City School District with whom I have worked closely over the years—Doris Bonfield, Bonnie Boothroy, Carolyn Duncan, Agelica Fotos, Linda Graham, Julia Hill, Mary Jepsen, Brian Lehman, Dianne McConahay, Martha Melton, Pat Tharp, and Marilyn Workman. And I can neither list nor thank enough all the teachers in the Iowa City Schools and the principals and staff at Lincoln Elementary School in Waterloo, Iowa, who have so graciously allowed me and my students to work in their classrooms.

Finally, I thank my family and my friends. My mother, Betty Lou Daniels, proofread for me. She is a loving, loyal mom. My husband, John Else, provided feedback as the manuscript was in progress and also love and support through many of the times when I was ready to give up the project. He has become my most valued reader. All my colleagues and friends were encouraging during those times, but I especially want to thank Jane Hansen, Linda Fielding, Bonnie Sunstein, Carolyn Colvin, and Kathy Whitmore for their encouragement. Without their support and examples I would never have persisted.

Introduction

R **EADING DISABLED,** learning disabled, dyslexic, mildly mentally disabled, communication disordered—the labels abound. Are so many of our children disabled? Why do we see disability rather than ability? Do we have narrow conceptions of "normal" literacy development? Is disabling instruction at fault? This book is the story of a summer reading program and the children it serves. In alternate summers I am responsible for the program, and I teach the children in the morning class. The children, viewed through the schooling system lens, are all "reading disabled." They range in age from 8 to 12 years and in reading ability from recognizing fewer than 15 words to reading at a late second or early third grade level. Some of the children are as many as five years behind "normal" reading development, whereas others are only two or three. Because the summer reading program classroom is not bound by school time schedules and the need to place children in grade-level classrooms, we emphasize children's abilities. We assume they can do many things, including learn to read, and we reject the labels—hence the term "struggling."

The summer reading program classroom is part of the longstanding University of Iowa Speech, Hearing, & Reading Clinic's Summer Residential Program, so we refer to it as SRP. Each summer between 20 and 30 children are in residence. Some have difficulties with speech, some with hearing, and usually half or more have reading difficulties. The children come to us via many routes: parents, teachers, school psychologists, grandparents, social services, and other university clinics refer the children to SRP. We select children from among those referred using an all-day screening process in the preceding spring. Usually between one-third and one-half of the children selected have participated in SRP the summer before. Most of the children participate for two or three summers.

The children live in groups of three to five with childcare workers in a dormitory. A licensed psychologist supervises the dormitory program. For the children, participating in the dorm program is like being at camp. The dorm staff is responsible for seeing to the physical and emotional well-being of the children. They also help the children with the social aspects of their various difficulties.

The children who participate primarily for reading attend class in the morning. In the afternoon, they have a small-group session to practice reading and writing, and they have an individual tutoring session. The individual tutors are graduate and undergraduate students in reading specialist or special education certification or endorsement programs.

SRP is the University of Iowa's primary practicum site for reading specialists. Since 1988 the underlying philosophy guiding all the reading instruction has been a "workshop" philosophy. (I will elaborate this in Chapter Three.) The reading program at SRP operates with a director (the faculty member in charge—in odd years Linda Fielding and in even years me), graduate assistants who supervise the individual tutoring sessions under the faculty member's direction and serve as classroom aides or small-group instructors, and administrative assistants.

For each child in SRP at least four reports are filed: a screening report, a dorm report, a classroom report, and a report of the individual tutoring sessions. The screening report summarizes previous records supplied to the clinic, presents the results of screening testing and interviews, and makes recommendations for the summer tutoring program. The other reports summarize the child's summer experience and make recommendations for future programming in the home and school settings. The reports are sent to parents and to any individuals or entities (such as the school) that parents request. In addition to these formal records, we also keep daily instructional records of individual, small-group, and classroom instruction.

At SRP all of us regularly study our practice. We observe tutoring sessions systematically, and students, visitors, and other staff are in and out of the morning classroom routinely. We require the graduate students to tape-record and listen to every individual tutoring session. We also have them transcribe portions of lessons regularly. I too tape-record and listen to myself and transcribe portions of my lessons. The examples used in this book are drawn from those tapes and other records of instruction from 1988 through 1994.

We learn a lot by studying ourselves—from both our successes and our failures. After seven years of running SRP with a workshop philosophy, we are hopeful about the potential that workshops offer for struggling readers. Although workshops are growing in popularity, their advantages for struggling readers are often overlooked. Many times, even when most literacy instruction is delivered in workshops, struggling readers are excluded from them. In this book, I want to share some of what we have learned about struggling readers in workshop classrooms.

Chapter One

Variable Children Need Variable Instruction

MY CLASSROOM is a workshop classroom. Workshop classrooms were developed first for writing instruction by Graves (1983). Hansen's book *When Writers Read* (1987) extended the concept to reading instruction. In both cases they were developed in "regular" classrooms for "regular" children; they were not designed as a special education service. I chose the workshop format because I believed the struggling readers I work with could learn in this "regular" setting. (I will explain my reasons in detail in Chapter Three.)

A workshop classroom operates a little like an art studio. After a short demonstration, students paint as their teacher circulates among them to help. The students learn to paint as they paint. In reading and writing workshops students learn to read and write as they read and write. This independent reading and writing is one essential feature of a workshop classroom. A second critical feature is choice. In workshops children choose the topics they write about and the books they read. In this way workshops take advantage of children's internal motivation and harness it for literacy learning. (I will talk more about choice throughout the book, but Chapter Four will treat it in depth.)

When observers enter a workshop classroom they are often confused because they see children scattered around the room doing a variety of different activities. The scene is quite different than classroom scenes of traditional literacy instruction, where most often there is a small group working with the teacher and the other children are sitting at desks working on assignments. A typical scene in my summer reading program (SRP) workshop classroom may look like this. Karen and I sit on the floor while she reads a new favorite book to me. Patrick squats beside us temporarily to listen to the story. He often browses through books about space and is quite proud of a piece he has written about the battleship U.S.S. *Iowa*. Randy stretches out on the rug in the center of the room and fills in his record form with the titles of a stack of books. He is proud of the many Story Box Series books he has read. Peter and Bobby meander along the bookshelves looking for some books that they can actually read and understand—books that are "just right" for them.

Later I join Andy and Jason at the desks by the windows as they wonder whether the plane in their book is a jet. They formed a close friendship during the summer and coauthored many science fiction books. As we talk several other children join us. One of them explains to me what a biplane is, and we decide that the plane is a propeller plane, not a jet. Peter and Bobby continue to meander along the bookshelves, and I worry that they are never going to find those "just right" books.

Several children choose to work alone all morning. Susan struggles trying to read a book about sharks that is quite difficult for her. But later in the summer, she shows us a shark book she compiled through her research. Mary reads about kangaroos; she is fascinated with marsupial reproduction and later shares the fact that baby kangaroos are called "Joeys" and that they have to crawl into the mother kangaroo's pouch. I decide to suggest several titles to Bobby. He's not happy with my choices nor with the fact that I am trying to choose for him. Peter is laboriously copying a section of his favorite book. I worry about this because I am fairly certain he cannot read what he is copying. Erin reads and rereads *Fortunately* by Remy Charlip. Later she will explain how practicing made this a "just right" book for her. Jimmy, Sammy, and Wes are each tucked into a corner and reading quietly. Now Karen moves over to Holly, and they work on a joint reading of Audrey Wood's *King Bidgood's in the Bathtub*, which they plan to share with the class later. Jamie works hard trying to read a James Marshall book. I'm concerned because I think it is probably too hard for him.

For the most part the children are engaged in their tasks. Throughout the morning, groups coalesce, break up, and form again. Single children stake out claims to the editing table or camp out under the supply table, areas of the classroom that will be explained in the next chapter. Others gather in small groups at student desks along the windows. I wander among them, talking with one child, then another. Sometimes I stop by a small group; at other times I read with a child or two. As often as not I sit on the rug in the center of the room for these conversations. I carry a spiral notebook and jot notes about the children's activities as I go.

THE CHILDREN

The descriptions of the children and their activities in the SRP classroom in the previous section are both accurate and deceptive. They are descriptions of actual children (pseudonyms are used) on a specific day, but they are deceptive in the picture of "normalcy" they convey. The descriptions would fit almost any workshop with any children, but these images clash with what I know of the children's school experiences. Before attending the summer reading program, all these children had been labeled, as I mentioned in the Introduction. From visits I made to their schools; talks with them, their teachers, and their parents; previous records; and a set of letters that 11 of the families wrote in response to my request for information about what school is like for children who have trouble reading, I know their school lives were a sharp contrast to the scene I just described. Here are comments from a just few of the students and their families.

Karen's mom wrote,

Karen's peer relationships have not been smooth. Kids seem to judge a peer's worth by school success at times (according to Karen). Since Karen had little success at school in the beginning she was the butt of jokes, rarely invited to join games or for overnights.

Patrick and his school classmates wrote,

School is not fun when you has trouble reading. It mades you mad. You don't get work done fast enough in class. It made you bored whin you cann't do the work. I made you feel dumb in class. It made you get a headake. It is stupit.

Randy, already 12 years old, did not know all his letters and did not seem to understand sound-letter relationships. His mother wrote, "I ask myself a lot, 'Why Randy?' Randy will never read at a high level."

Peter had been in special education classes through his whole school career. His mother remembered, "The anger in your son's eyes when he wants so badly to do something on his own but can't due to his difficulty in reading. The list could go on and on."

Bobby's mom wrote, "This is really a hard letter to write to you because there is really nothing positive to say. Bobby doesn't feel comfortable with reading." She reported that he does not like her friend's daughter because "she is smart and she can read."

Andy dictated, "I always say to myself, 'I am dumb,' and hit myself in the head. Sometimes I wish I could die, but my Mom doesn't like that."

Mary's mom told a story of a two-year journey to get some help for her daughter. She commented, "Times can be very difficult for someone who cannot seem to keep up with those around them. It even gets worse when you have a sister who is 13 months younger than you and she loves to read books to you."

Jimmy told a story of a man who came to his school and gave a seven-page test. The teacher asked the man if she could read it to the children who had trouble reading, but he said no. Jimmy was concerned that the man was not going to know what he knew. The man would think he was stupid.

Jamie's foster parents wrote, "Jamie would frequently talk to us about how he could not read like the other kids. When they did workbook pages, they would finish three and he didn't finish one. He wondered why his teacher never called on him to read out loud because he always raised his hand. As time progressed, he became more of a discipline problem and his self-concept went even lower."

Although the SRP children were not learning to read in their schools, my intent is not to fix the blame on the children, their parents, nor their teachers. The fault was not the children's. The children can learn to read. Neither was the fault the parents'. I have met, corresponded, and talked with the children's parents; they are good parents. The children's teachers were not at fault either. I visited the children's schools and observed their teachers; I saw good teachers. The fault lies beyond these particular children, these particular parents, and these particular schools. The fault belongs to general organizational patterns for delivering reading instruction.

VARIABILITY NOT DISABILITY

To make the SRP classroom work, we have had to overcome the children's deep and abiding prejudices against reading, against books, and against themselves. The classroom works because it assumes that children's abilities vary. Because children are variable the classroom accommodates variability. Choice is the mechanism for accommodation. When children choose their activities within a structured environment, they are able to choose tasks consistent with their abilities and interests. Thus, there is no need for them to be "disabled." Rather than view children as capable or disabled, workshop classrooms assume that children are different, that each child is unique and has unique interests and abilities, and that differences are normal. In addition, because the children are multiaged and because a certain proportion of the children return every year, the SRP classroom can take advantage of the fact that some students already have learned the classroom routines. The experienced SRP students help the children who are new learn the routines and expectations, and the variation in ability means that often children can help one another.

Most schools make different assumptions. They are organized by grades, and all the children of a particular age are assigned to a particular grade. Each child spends a single year in a particular classroom with a particular teacher. The school curriculum is organized likewise by grades. Textbooks are grade specific. All the children are expected to learn the curriculum for that grade from the grade-level textbooks provided. Each year the children progress to a new grade, which means a new classroom and a new teacher. The underlying assumption is that children who are the same age have the same abilities and can benefit from the same instruction.

Nothing could be farther from the truth—particularly in literacy development. In almost any classroom organized only by chronological age, the range of reading and writing ability is very wide. It is not uncommon to have both first and sixth grade classrooms that include children who cannot read at all and children who can read almost anything. Some children read and write before they come to kindergarten; others cannot read and write when they leave high school. Some children learn a word after it seeing it only once; others fail to recognize a word after as many as 70 encounters with it.

Because variability in literacy learning is a constant concern for educators, many solutions have been developed over the years. In the United States the predominant one from the 1950s through the 1980s in the elementary schools was ability grouping. Teachers used three different textbooks for reading instruction: one for the low group, one for the middle group, and one for the high group. However, even this did not solve the problem. Within groups, the variability was still too wide. There were always children who did not fit any group.

Through the 1970s and 1980s remedial and special education programs proliferated. Children who did not fit the classroom groups were pulled out of their classrooms to receive special help. Unfortunately, the record for such pull-out programs is not good. U.S. national evaluations of Chapter 1 remedial reading programs conclude that positive effects are at best small and often nonexistent. There is no comparable national data for special education programs, but the data that exist are equally discouraging (Walmsley & Allington, 1995). The programs may actually result in less instructional time for the children served because some classroom teachers view their literacy learning as the responsibility of the special education teacher or reading specialist. In addition, the segregation of children by ability stigmatizes and leads to detrimental emotional responses that destroy the children's motivation. The segregation contributes to what Stanovich (1986) dubbed the "Matthew Effect" after the scripture in the Bible that refers to the rich growing richer while the poor grow poorer.

The overwhelming response to the evaluations of remedial and special education programs has been to dismantle reading groups in classrooms and to call for alternative programs that do not segregate children from their peers. Many classrooms now deliver reading instruction to all children from one textbook and have specialists work within classrooms in "push-in," rather than "pull-out," programs that promote inclusion. Walmsley and Allington (1995) have adopted the following statement as a principle for reform: "All children are entitled to the same literacy experiences, materials, and expectations." Often these authors' comments make it seem that segregated instruction has been entirely responsible for children's failures in learning to read: "If it is true that the major differences between the literacy strategies of better and poorer students can be explained by differences in curriculum, opportunities, and instructional tasks, then there should be no barriers to entitling all children to the same literacy experiences and expectations" (p. 29).

While I, too, believe that segregated instruction contributes to reading failure and does little to teach children to read, I do not believe that homogenized instruction will eliminate reading failure. We must remember that ability grouping and special pull-out programs arose as a solution to the real problem of variability in children's acquisition of literacy. To return to uniform instruction, uniform materials, and uniform expectations is unrealistic. Variability exists. To pretend that it does not is to invite another decade or two of failure in literacy learning. We cannot return to systems that ignore variability because one method of accommodation failed; rather we must explore new ways of accommodating variability. Variability will not disappear because remedial and special education programs failed.

Workshop classrooms are a positive response to variability because classroom activities and routines apply to all children and are not delineated by children's abilities. The activities accommodate a wide range of instructional materials, so workshop classrooms accommodate a wide range of children. They can easily serve multiage, multiability groups. They do not segregate children by ability either within or outside the classroom. Although every child is expected to participate in each of the workshop activities—reading, writing, sharing, and talking in conferences—each chooses the materials to use and the content on which to focus. When children are free to choose their own instructional topics and materials, they can choose suitably. Their choices can accommodate their abilities rather than define them as "disabled." While choice and workshops are not magic panaceas (I will talk about problems with choice in Chapter Four), they are a promising alternative for reorganizing the delivery of literacy instruction.

In School Classrooms

Workshop classrooms were developed for school classrooms, and there are many resources available that describe their implementation. These include *Writing: Teachers and Children at Work* by Graves (1983), *When Writers Read* by Hansen (1987), Atwell's *In the Middle: Writing, Reading, and Learning with Adolescents* (1987), and *Read On: A Conference Approach to Reading* (1986a) and *Write On: A Conference Approach to Writing* (1986b) by Hornsby, Sukarna, and Parry. My intent in this book is to show how and why the workshop approach should be used for all children, even those—especially those—who are struggling readers and writers.

Chapter Two

Workshop Classrooms Make Space and Time for Variability

THE CLASSROOM SPACE

The summer reading program classroom is like many other classrooms. It has four walls, a bank of windows, chalkboards, bookshelves, student desks, children, and a teacher. The classroom is wide open and everything centers around a rug in the middle, as Figure 1 on the next page shows. There is no teacher's desk, and children's desks and tables are located at the periphery. There are not enough desks for every child; instead, each has a plastic container that holds his or her materials. The containers are stored on shelves near the entryway. On the other side of the door is an editing table. Bookshelves and milk crates filled with books are interspersed along the walls. At the far end of the room there is a supply table with paper, pencils, pens, crayons, glue, rulers, and scissors.

The rug at the center of the classroom is the gathering place for large-group sessions. The student desks, arranged singly and in small clusters, accommodate small-group and individual activities. The setup is simple and flexible. We can all focus on a single speaker when we gather at the rug, but we can work in small groups or by ourselves when we disperse for workshop. The classroom does not need to be rearranged for various types of activities. It can accommodate our choices of the moment.

I learned that a simple, flexible physical space was important the first time we used a workshop format for instruction at SRP 1988. I observed Jan Schmitt-Craven, at the time a graduate student, as she taught in the classroom. We learned a lot that first time through. Our classroom setup was complex. We

Figure 1   The Summer Reading Program Workshop Classroom

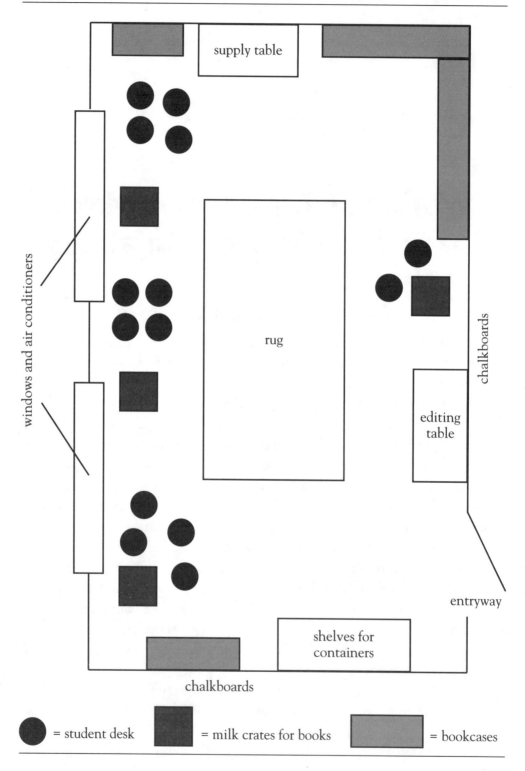

had a listening center, a small-group area, a partner reading area, individual desks, a large-group area, and editing and supply tables. We created the separate large-group area by surrounding the rug (donated by Jan's relatives) with bookcases. Colorful pillows and bean-bag chairs (also donated by Jan's relatives) made this area more inviting. This complex arrangement was confusing to manage. When faced with so many alternatives, the children did not function well. They bickered about who would be at what station and about who would get the pillows and the bean-bag chairs. At the listening center the tape recorders were continually breaking down. Children were stumbling over cords, and tape recorders were falling off the card table. We did not want to put an elaborate management system into place to regulate the children's use of the various stations. We knew choice was important and we wanted the children to choose. Unfortunately, choice frequently resulted in arguing. Eventually, Jan, who is the most determined person I have ever known, got that classroom running smoothly—but with considerable effort. We decided that we simply had too much going on in too small a space. We realized that we could not put every good idea we had heard or read about to work in our classroom; and we certainly could not incorporate them all at the beginning.

The wide variety of books and other reading materials located at the periphery of the room are the essence of the classroom. Wide means a *very* wide range. I have many books at the preprimer level, and I have sophisticated nonfiction books about sharks, cars, and other topics. I place the books at the edges of the room in a lot of different areas so that the children do not converge at a single spot when it is time to select books. Sometimes teachers feel that books should be arranged by level of difficulty so that children can find suitable books more easily. Others feel that putting all the easy books in one place makes it obvious who is reading easy books, and they think that children avoid the easy books because they are embarrassed or choose harder books because of their prestige. These teachers feel that books should be arranged by content, for example animals, sports, cartoons, riddles, mysteries, and so forth, and that a range of difficulty should be available in each genre. I eventually settled on a combination of the two arrangements. Most of the books in our classroom are arranged in categories, but there are several places where children can go to find very easy books. I did this because the children were having trouble finding easy books and asked me to put them aside in a particular place. However, this request came well into the workshop when the children had developed a solid community and felt comfortable and safe in the classroom. (See also Chapter Four about choosing books.)

THE CLASSROOM TIME

In the SRP workshop, I use a set of basic activities that occur at regular times—group talk, oral literature, minilessons, reading, writing, and sharing (see Figure 2)—which I will explain in the following sections. The activities are broad, generic ones in which all children, regardless of the level of their literacy ability, can participate. We begin the day talking together on the rug in the center of the classroom, and then I read to the children. Next we move into the reading workshop. The workshop has a three-part structure: (1) minilesson (group), (2) reading, and (3) sharing (group). In the first group session I do a brief minilesson, then the children disperse to read independently for about 30 minutes. As the children read I circulate among them to hold brief conferences and help children with specific problems. To close the workshop, we gather together as a group and share our activities with one another. Usually three or four children take the "sharer's chair" and talk about a book they have read. One child may read an entire short book to the class; another may share a favorite page or illustration. Each child invites classmates' responses by asking, "Comments or questions?" Sometimes I make a comment or ask a question as well. After the reading workshop we go to recess, and after recess student volunteers read to small groups of children. We end our day with the writing workshop, which functions similar to the reading workshop. I enjoy the mornings. Reading and writing with these children is fun.

Figure 2   SRP Morning Classroom Schedule

9:00–9:10	Group talk
9:10–9:20	Oral literature
9:20–10:15	Reading workshop Minilesson Independent reading Reading sharing
10:15–10:30	Recess
10:30–10:50	Oral literature (small groups)
10:50–11:40	Writing workshop Minilesson Independent writing Writing sharing

The consistency of daily activities is an important feature of the SRP workshop classroom. The consistency allows the children to take control of their own reading and writing activities. They know that they do not have to begin and finish activities in specified time blocks. If they have not finished reading a book or writing a story, they will have time to finish it the next day or the one after that. Because the time schedule is consistent, children can plan how they will allot the time. Planning allows them to take responsibility for their own learning.

We spend the whole morning reading and writing. I cannot emphasize enough the importance of long, regularly scheduled, uninterrupted blocks of time. Hansen (1987) has probably summarized the time issues best. Reading and writing take time. During vacations I probably read seven or eight books. I buy them with excitement knowing that I have seven or so open free days with no demands on my time. Knowing that I have time allows me to immerse myself in the world of books. I don't have to keep bouncing between the book world and my own. Writing takes time, too. It is even harder to pop in and out of a writing world. To write this book I scheduled three hours every day (and sometimes more) during which the book would be my only focus. Children need time for these activities, too. They have trouble popping in and out of worlds. They need extended time that they can count on. Writing and reading don't always settle themselves into neat and tidy little half-hour spaces, but if children know that there will be series of spaces that they can count on regularly then they can plan their reading and writing over a longer period of time.

Another advantage to using a consistent set of activities in the workshop is that after my initial teaching, the children can do the activities independently. This leaves me free to focus on individuals. I do not have to spend a lot of time planning what we do each day because most of what we do is controlled by routines. As a result, I can spend my time observing and thinking about children. The structured activities release me and allow me to know each child's uniqueness, which I will discuss later in this chapter after I explain the classroom activities in more detail.

Group Talk

Ten minutes of unstructured group talk begins the day. We talk about what we have been doing since we saw one another last. For example, we have talked about "wally" ball (a game played on handball courts), an Indiana Jones movie, running over a cowpie on your bike, the moral lessons to be learned when one child kicked a chipmunk, rules for having a better discussion, and things we can do to get along better. Sometimes there will be an issue that I really want to talk about, such as some children's refusal to cooperate with two others who wanted to make a book about what kinds of cars their classmates would drive in the future. Because cooperation and helping one another are major themes in our classroom, I took the group time to talk about this. Sometimes the children are spontaneous and talk excitedly. At other times they are quiet and need to be drawn out with questions. This varies by day and by child.

Andy's story about his snake was typical of the spontaneity in group talk. He explained that he used to have a snake but he had to give it away because it ate one of his gerbils. Several us could not believe what we heard and questioned, "What?" and "Your snake ate your gerbil?" But Karen, the naturalist, immediately wanted to know whether the snake was black with yellow stripes on it because black with yellow stripes is bad. Holly couldn't believe that Andy would keep a snake in the house, and Andy tried to explain that it was a pet. Mary wanted to know if it bit.

At this point I reined them in a little and suggested that Andy answer Karen's question about the color of the snake. It was white and gray. But the children still wanted to know if it bit, and Andy said that it had bitten him once. Mary said she had had a pet like that once.

Then the conversation shifted to the gerbil, and once again Karen was full of facts about gerbils—how they differed from hamsters and mice and how they sometimes ate their babies. The exchange continued with me and several other children sharing their snake experiences.

When a child clearly wants to share something I try to maintain a space for that sharing. However, some of the children are much less certain and confident of their interaction in the large-group setting. Often Bobby, John, Randy, and initially Mary participated only when specific questions about their activities the day before were directly addressed to them. I accepted and responded to their brief contributions as well as to their classmates' longer ones. I wanted them to be comfortable.

When I first introduced group talk, I wondered if I was just wasting time. Ten minutes of unstructured talk might seem to have no point. However, the longer we had the group talk, the more important I decided it was. I realized that this time period played a very important part in building the sense of community that is so important in workshop classrooms. This unstructured time is crucial to our getting to know and trust one another. It is also a time when reading and writing problems can be left aside while children share their strengths with classmates. Because it is time for talking, there are no right and wrong answers and the children are the experts on the topics they introduce. It is a time when their competence is spotlighted.

Oral Literature

During the oral literature session, I read to the children—sometimes my choice or the children's, sometimes a story or an informational text. This 10 minutes and the 20 minutes following recess are scheduled because it is important for the children to learn what reading is by seeing it modeled well. During this time, the children experience reading as meaning getting. Often they talk to understand. For example, on one occasion I was reading an attractive picture book about sharks. One section is about a shark who bit a young boy and then would not let go of his leg. The text says that the shark had been wounded, and it was now weak because the wounds were not completely healed. I commented, "That doesn't seem to make sense to me. If it was so weak, how come they didn't get it to let go of the boy's leg?"

In the discussion that followed several children offered explanations. Jimmy suggested that it was because the shark was so hungry, and Patrick wondered why it didn't have the power to bite hard. Peter suggested that when sharks hear people swimming they bite and they don't let go. Karen thought it might be something like when you have held onto your pencil too long and the muscles just freeze. She suggested it might be like when we chew our food.

In these oral literature discussions, I encourage talk that is aimed at getting meaning from the text because good talk makes good thinking visible. Children who have not had opportunities to participate in and listen to talk about books sometimes think reading is a mystical process, and they do not understand how readers move from words to meaning. Talk during and after book reading is valuable. However, on some occasions the children sit mesmerized and spellbound, caught up in the tale. A variety of types of participation—from attentive listening to enthusiastic talk—are possible, and I try to value each child's way of participating. Ways of participating vary from book to book and child to child.

Reading Workshop

For the next 55 minutes, we have reading workshop. During this time, we follow a group-read-group structure, which is explained in the following sections.

Minilessons

In the first group session, we meet for a short time (usually 5, but always less than 10 minutes) and have a minilesson (Calkins, 1986). I use this time to introduce new ideas or work on skills that the children seem to need. For example, one day I wanted to show the children how to make better use of the time they spent with their "dream" books (books that they were interested in but could not actually read). I began the lesson like this:

> Today I want to show you something you can do with a dream book. Remember, I'm sort of a fuss budget—fuss budget—and I worry all the time because you spend too much time in your dream books and you don't read enough easy books, and I want you to read lots and lots of easy books? Well, actually, you've been finding some good things to do with your dream books. Susan, would you like to tell us how you used your dream book when you wrote about sharks?

We reviewed how Susan had used her book to get information to put in her shark book. Then I continued to explain a technique, using the tape recorder, that would actually help the children read a favorite part of their dream book. The lesson introduced a possibility. I later followed up with individual children who chose to try the technique.

Independent Reading

After the lesson the children disperse to read. They choose their own books and their own activities connected to their reading. Many of the children sit quietly and read. Others partner read—one child reads a book to another child, or the two take turns reading various parts. Sometimes a small group reads a comic book, works on reading a selection from the *Guinness Book of World Records*, or reads a play from multiple copies of an old basal reader. Occasionally, a child does some writing related to a book he or she has read. There are certain places in the classroom for quiet reading and certain places where talk related to reading is allowed. Choice gives the setting flexibility. The variety of activities and materials makes it possible for each child to use the time productively.

During this time, I circulate among the children. Each day I focus on three to five children, and I have individual conferences with them. The conferences are about what the child is reading, and the first focus of the conference is the content of the book. In addition, I concentrate on the child's particular needs. I identify the needs by asking the child what he or she is working on or by recalling previous interactions I have had with the child during conferences, lessons, and group times. In the early conferences, there is a lot of discussion about choosing books. Until the children can do this, not much can happen in a reading workshop. After this initial stage, the content of the conferences varies greatly, depending on the books the children choose and the goals that they set for themselves. I take notes as I circulate. At the end of the independent reading time, the children record their activities. Over the years my notetaking system has evolved to the one I will talk about in Chapter Eight.

Reading Sharing

At 10:00 we come back to the rug for reading sharing. The children take turns sharing their reading with one another. Most days between three and five children share. Usually a child tells the title of his or her book, gives reasons for choosing or liking the book, and provides a brief summary. The child then asks for questions and comments and directs a short discussion of the book. I participate as another discussant. Wes, one of the more advanced readers, shared a book about sunken treasure:

> It's about, um, how they um find treasure and stuff like that and and the [unintelligible] of it is about this one ship. I can't remember what it's called. Anyway they have lots of gold and jewels and silver, everything like that and it sunk in a storm. And and then Spain, they wanted the—they wanted the treasure back so they. [brief interruption] So they, Spain, they wanted the treasure back so they sent people down to get as much treasure as they could find. [brief interruption] And then it shows after the years gone by and around the 1960s they said, they sent some people down to look for it. They thought they found it, but it just—they found some other stuff and it was all in place and what they had was some jets blow air down and it makes a hole in the sand.

At this Jimmy remarked, "Cool!" Wes continued, "And they were a hundred miles off from where they were supposed to be digging and they finally found it. That was in 1971."

Sammy interrupted with the question, "This was in 19 what?" and he and Wes worked out the length of time between the original effort and the successful one. This was followed by a discussion with Wes, Susan, and Karen about what was actually found. The reading sharing provided a time for children to work together in constructing meaning.

Recess and More Oral Literature

Recess follows the reading workshop, and after recess we meet for a small-group oral literature session. I break the children into three groups of five, and I and adult volunteers (usually university students) read to them. We do this so that the children have more opportunity to engage with both the text and the adult reading the text. The talk is similar to the talk that occurs in the first oral literature session, only there is more of it.

Writing Workshop

At 10:50 we move into the writing workshop. We use a group-write-group structure, similar to the reading workshop. We meet for a short lesson, write, and then meet again for sharing. Minilessons focus on writing topic choice, revision, use of quotation marks—whatever it is that the children seem to need instruction on at a particular time. The followup to the lessons occurs in the individual conferences and during the writing sharing. For example, in one workshop session, several children copied segments of other people's writing into their own stories. When they commented on what they had done, I asked if they had used quotation marks. Later I did a short minilesson about using quotation marks. The issue came up again during sharing. At one sharing time I drew the children's attention to the quotation marks. On another occasion, Erin explained to the class during sharing, "Right here, the part that I read, I copied out of the book, and I put, um, quotation marks. It doesn't...look right here. I put his name down here because I wrote what he thinks."

Sharing time in writing is time when children learn from one another. For example, one of the problems the children in my classroom have had was writing stories that they thought were long enough to publish. (Publishing in our classroom means having an edited manuscript typed, illustrated, and bound in a cover using a plastic spiral.) The solutions to the length problem came from the children themselves. If a story was too short one popular solution was to publish a book of short stories. Karen had another solution: she had a dog story and a horse story that she decided to combine into one story. She explained to the other children:

> Um, you won't be able to hear the beginning 'cause I'm starting right in the middle. The two sheets in the middle. I'm gonna start from where she's doing dog stuff. Um, and I fed him and walked him but Dad said, "He will get old and he will die." So after a few years, he died and I, and I was very sad and I cried myself to sleep. The next day I asked my Dad if I could have a horse. Dad said, "Yes, you can, if you, if it is OK with your mom."
> "It is. I know it is. I know it is."
> "Yes, you can," Dad said, "but there is a lot of work to do. I will help you."
> And this is where it starts combining together. "Horses are nice. They run, jump...."

In recent years we have moved from a writing workshop to a topic workshop. I will explain this change in detail in Chapter Seven.

The Afternoon

When writing sharing is over, our classroom day is done. The children return their books and writing to their containers, line up, and go to lunch at their dormitory. After lunch, they return to SRP for a 45-minute small-group session and a 45-minute individual tutoring session. The small-group time includes another oral literature session, sustained silent reading, and sustained silent writing. The tutoring sessions, like the classroom, use children's trade books and the writing children are currently working on as instructional materials. They also reflect the belief that if children are to learn to read and write, they must read and write.

The structure of the tutoring sessions varies for individual children, and the sessions become more variable as the summer progresses. However, there are two basic formats—one for children who are emergent readers and one for beginning readers who read above a first grade level (as measured by an informal reading inventory). The structure of these sessions has evolved over the years and, as those familiar with Reading Recovery (Clay, 1993) will note, has been influenced by reading Marie Clay's work. The sessions now include the following activities:

1. rereading of familiar books
2. diagnostic recording
3. writing
4. editing
5. focus on specific objectives
6. book introduction
7. reading a new book

The tutoring sessions provide heavy doses of direct instruction in the context of actual reading and writing. I believe that individual tutoring is necessary for these children until they develop a large enough sight vocabulary (words recognized instantly) to read books that are not written with a severely restricted vocabulary. In terms of traditional grade levels, this is probably when the children reach a late first or early second grade reading level. When the children reach this level, their sight vocabulary in combination with the reading strategies they have learned will allow them to read books successfully and independently. At this point they become what Clay (1985) has labeled "a self-improving system."

PAYING ATTENTION TO VARIABILITY

In this section I will show how the general activity structures allow me to respond to the children's individual needs. The first step in individualizing instruction is to teach children general routines that will eventually allow them to work independently. As I taught my students the structure of the workshop classroom and noted how they responded, I became acquainted with each of them in all their uniqueness. To begin, I wrote a daily schedule on a poster. I gave an overview of the day—brief explanations of what to do at a particular time—and explained that it was all right if the children did not understand completely what to do. Every time we began a new activity, I explained. Early lessons focused on procedures as the following excerpt from the first day shows.

> Roller: OK. Now, it's time, we just finished our group, right? That's what this says up here [pointing to the schedule]. And now we're going into reading workshop. And we start reading workshop with another group, just a short group, and in that we have some sort of a lesson and this is a particularly important time to everybody and paying attention. Then we'll read and then we'll have group again and we'll have some sharing. Now today our lesson is going to be about procedures, OK, what we do in this classroom. That's what procedures are. Susan, you can use one of those little carpets to put under you if you want to so you don't have to sit on the floor. You need one too? OK, you're OK. Um. Let's see. Where was I? Oh, we're in procedures today and I just did the first part of it. In reading workshop we have group, then we read, then we have group. Can you tell me back what we do in reading workshop? We have group we do—we go read, and then we have group. Say it again. What do we do in reading workshop? Group, read, group.

> Children: Group, read, group.

Following this introduction, the lesson moved on to the things the children would have to do in order to make the classroom structure work. Much of the discussion was about how to choose books. Several children who had taken part in the workshop the previous year explained that there were three kinds of books: kinda easy, just right, and kinda hard. They said that everybody has these three kinds of books and that during the workshop children should spend most of their time reading kinda easy and just right books. After the topic of book selection, the discussion moved to activities that were acceptable during reading workshop. I carefully explained to the children what I expected them to do. For activities that were new to the children, such as reading sharing, I modeled the task, explaining as I demonstrated each step. First, I explained how the children would keep track of their sharing turns by moving a clip labeled with their name from a clipboard marked "have not shared" to a clipboard marked "have shared":

> When I share, we'll take the clip off here and we'll put it over here [from the board marked "have not shared" to the board marked "have shared"], and this says, "reading, have shared." OK. Now, when you share, come up to the front, wait until all the children are sitting up, wait until all the things are put in the tubs, everything's clean, wait until every child's eyes are on you. Because...[their] job is to listen during sharing. OK, when everybody's eyes are now on me, so I'm ready to share my book today. I'm just going to share this because you've heard it before,

so it'll help you know what to do. OK. I'm going to share *The Beast in Ms. Rooney's Room* and it's by Patricia Riley Giff.

There was some discussion about the cover, then I continued.

> OK, so I'm gonna share this book. Now what you do, first you tell the title like I did. You tell the author and then you say why you like this book, why you chose it. I chose this book because I think it has a great story and because I love the way Patricia Riley Giff describes. She just does so good at making you see people. For example, and I'm going to read to you a couple of my favorite parts. It's only gonna take a minute. For example, I like the part where she describes Matthew: "Matthew had stick-out ears and a wet-the-bed smell." I mean, can't you just see Matthew? And I also like it, um, when she's still talking about Matthew, "Matthew grinned at Richard. His teeth were big and curled on the ends." I like that part, too. Must have funny teeth. So that's why I like this book. Comments and questions? Now this is your job. You have to tell me what you liked about what I said.

As I taught procedures and observed the children's responses I took notes. The notes helped me decide what to do next. After the first day I sorted the children into one of three categories: doing fine, having trouble, seem fine but I don't know. For example, my notes on Sammy and Mary indicated they were doing fine, as the following excerpt shows. (R indicates notes from reading; W indicates notes from writing.)

Sammy

> R: *Boats and Ships* by Susan Harris. Sammy was off by himself and not interacting much. I checked him on book choice—This was a little hard, but mostly he was missing proper names, he was using correct initial consonants.

> W: Sammy went right to work. Stayed on task whole time. Did page and a half draft on Nintendo. Pretty readable.

Mary

> R: Mary was reluctant to join in introductions. After that she took off. I helped her with her folder and she caught right on. Read several books. Really read them too!

> W: Got right down to writing. Shared Tiger story.

On the other hand my notes for Andy and Randy suggested they may have been having trouble:

Andy

> R: *Shake My Sillies Out* [Raffi] He had chosen this as a just right. It was way too hard. He called [the word] "shake" [the words] "sleep" and "smoke." Was missing most of the words. I directed him to the SB [Story Box Series] books. He was pleased. Read straight through *In a*

Dark, Dark Wood [Cowley & Melser] aloud to his buddies. I commented on how the repetition helped.

W: Working on a story with Jason—Jason Life.

Randy

R: *City in the Summer* [Schick]. Checked for book choice. This was way too hard. Ms. P helped him with SB books. He found four that he could read.

W: Ms. P worked with him. Said he was having a tough time. I sat with him. Showed him how to use the spider book to write about spiders.

Notes on several of the children indicate that I simply did not know very much about what they were doing:

Peter

R: Peter was excited and enthusiastic. He was the bathroom tour guide. I did not get to him during reading.

W: Ms. P worked with him on scribble pictures.

Jimmy

R: Haven't gotten to Jimmy.

W: Didn't get to Jimmy.

Bobby

R: Didn't get to Bobby.

W: He sat with Ms. P stayed on the outskirts of the circle—seemed not to be joining in.

From the notes it was clear that book choice was an issue for some of the children and was something I needed to watch. I also needed to monitor the children whom I had not observed closely. There were several children who seemed to be on track and productive and did not need my immediate attention. Based on what happened the first day, I decided simply to remind children about procedures and choosing books in the minilessons and to continue to follow up on the procedure lessons and the book choices in the individual conferences.

By the end of the first week a pretty complete picture of the children emerged. It was clear that Mary and Sammy were independent workers who would continue to be engaged and productive. Several other children were in this category. However, several of the children who had had difficulty that first day continued to have difficulty, and several who had escaped my scrutiny the first day seemed to be masters at doing relatively little in quiet, productive-looking ways. For example, here are my first week's reading notes on Bobby:

6/20 *Corvette* [Koblenz] Dream. He identified this, said he put the easy books away 'cause they weren't neat. Sent him back for easy and JR [just right] books.

6/21 Was reading Rigby Education space book. First page he didn't get many words right—but then he looked at pictures and worked on it and did better. Most mistakes were meaningful. I encouraged him to reread. Was looking at aircraft [book] again—identified as Dream Book.

6/22 Got carrying and launch pad from space shuttle Rigby book—sent him to get really easy books. Got *The Bulldozer Cleared the Way* [Rigby Education].

6/23 Still looking at *Corvette* book. No easy books.

Bobby was resisting reading easy books. If left to himself he would spend the whole period looking at books that were too difficult for him. Although none of the other children had this consistent a pattern, my notes for many of them included a comment or two about inappropriate book choices. I needed to give more instruction about book choice. In fact, this is a problem that we have struggled with every year. Chapter Four deals with this issue in depth.

Notes on some of the other children began to give a picture of what skills the children might need to learn. For example, my notes on Andy follow:

Fiddle-Dee-Dee [Melser] JR—maybe a little hard. He was reading nonsense—but was getting initial consonant sounds. When I asked if it made sense he went back and corrected—he said "said" for "sheep" and "got" for "goats."

This overreliance on graphophonic information and lack of attention to meaning showed up for several children, which suggested that lessons emphasizing the use meaning for word recognition might be useful. My notes for Karen indicated she was strong in this area and could be used as a model:

6/20 *Hi, Dog!* [Adams, Hartson, & Taylor] JR. Did well except for names. We discussed using letter strategy for names. She used the strategy independently later in the paragraph. She self-corrected after calling [the word] "went" [the word] "want"—used meaning cues.

I might ask her to help me with a minilesson on these strategies. Or perhaps I could encourage her to talk about the strategy during sharing. Her difficulty with proper nouns was one that often stops less able readers in their tracks. I suggested a strategy I use in reading Russian novels: I simply use the first letter of the character's name to refer to the character.

This sampling of notes from the first week should help explain how teachers find out—through careful observation, notetaking, and reflection—what to teach in their workshop classrooms. When children have the opportunity to do real reading and writing, and they have an observant teacher who tries to lead by watching what they are doing and helping them move forward with what they want to do, the skills that need to be taught become apparent and the workshop offers an ideal setting for teaching them. Minilessons on using meaning in word recognition, choosing appropriate books, and a simple strategy for pronouncing proper names would all make sense based on my first week's observations.

Over the years, the skills and strategies that the SRP children need to learn seem to become apparent again and again and in a relatively stable sequence. This is probably because from year to year we select children with similar profiles. As a result, I now approach the summer with a set of four basic goals for the children:

1. Read a lot.
2. Choose good books.
3. Use good strategies.
4. Make reading make sense.

As this book progresses each of these goals will take on more meaning. However, it is important to realize that I did not begin with goals. The goals emerged as I worked with the children. Each year I find I change the goals a little, and there is always a child or two who does not fit the framework. I try to keep the goals broad so a wide variety of activities will fit them. I am always guarding against fitting children to goals instead of fitting goals to children.

In School Classrooms

Workshops in school classrooms function in ways similar to the SRP workshops I have described. They have a basic set of activities that include, at a minimum, independent self-selected reading, writing, and sharing. However, teachers may vary in whether they hold conferences with individuals or small groups, whether they do sharing in small or large groups, and how they incorporate oral reading into the workshop. Sometimes they break the workshop routine to do a themed unit or a play or some other literacy activity. Sometimes they integrate the workshop with science and social studies activities and themes. The variations are plentiful and depend on the particular teacher and particular children involved. However, there are several issues that come up frequently in my conversations with teachers about what works for them.

Time is a big issue in school classrooms. In the summer classroom daily time is not a problem because we have the whole morning and no one to answer to but ourselves. For school classroom teachers, it's not as easy. When I talk to them and say that 45 minutes to an hour each day should be allotted for each workshop and that I wouldn't bother to start a workshop if I couldn't have it that long for at least three days a week, they generally react by saying they couldn't possibly find that much time. Yet most of the teachers I know teach reading every day for a substantial block of time. They also devote time to the language arts textbook, spelling, and oral literature. When they add it all up, they find that they are spending as much as 450 to 600 minutes a week on reading and language arts instruction. They probably can find 225 to 450 minutes per week for a reading and writing workshop, but they will have to give up some of the activities they are currently doing and change the way they do others so that activities are consistent with workshop structures and philosophies. The workshop is not something that can be added onto an already full language arts program.

Another problem in the regular classroom is availability of materials. The classroom must be supplied with many materials that range widely in topic, genre, and difficulty level. Samuel's comments are relevant here. I talked with him about how SRP was helping him because I wanted him to be aware of the strategies he was learning. I suggested that it was Samuel's newly acquired strategies that were helping him. He contradicted me immediately by saying, "No. I had the strategies. My school didn't have books I could read. SRP helps me because there are so many good, easy books that I can read."

Some classroom teachers, particularly intermediate-level teachers, have also told me that they cannot use the workshop all the time because they do not have enough easy books. As I mentioned, in almost any elementary classroom, there will be some children who either are not reading or just barely reading and others who can read almost anything. If we supply our workshop classrooms with a narrow range of books that someone thinks is suitable for a particular age group, we defeat the purpose. *Every* classroom should have the easiest picture books on the shelves as well as some challenging novels and nonfiction. If we look at the tremendous budgets for expensive textbooks, which are of questionable use to many children, we see plenty of money available for trade books. We simply must give up the notion that every child must have a copy of the single texts we choose for instruction. We must refocus the expenditure on improving classroom and school libraries.

Another issue for teachers in school classrooms is which children should be included in the workshop. I have seen teachers who run workshops for children of regular abilities and run a separate program for struggling readers. I cannot disagree with this strongly enough. Struggling readers can learn in a workshop setting. *All children can learn in a system that respects their abilities.*

Chapter Three

Why Create Workshop Classrooms for Struggling Readers?

I **DECIDED** to use a workshop classroom in the summer reading program because I was dissatisfied. I had lost confidence in traditional approaches to teaching reading and was attracted to the philosophical underpinnings of workshop teaching.

DISSATISFACTIONS

After working with struggling readers for nearly 20 years in public school and university clinic settings, I was not happy with the results. Most of the readers I worked with continued to struggle no matter what I did. I first encountered these readers when I taught tenth grade English in a rural high school in Ohio. I was astounded at the number of students who could not enjoy books I loved because they could not read them. Within the year I enrolled in my first graduate reading course to learn how I could better teach these students to read. My next position was in a large urban high school in Oklahoma. I taught remedial reading and completed a Master of Arts degree in reading in 1975. Then I decided high school was much too late to attend to reading problems. Thus, my next position was as an elementary reading specialist in a school in Montana serving children of military personnel. However, even at this level the extra small-group work for approximately half an hour a day did not seem to work. The children who began the year as struggling readers, although they met their objectives and passed their skills tests, ended the year as struggling readers, and the same children received reading services year after year.

In 1977 I returned to school again for a doctorate degree, hoping that it would help me understand struggling readers and how to teach them. I completed the Ph.D. and came to the University of Iowa as a reading educator. As part of my assignment, I was in charge of SRP. Here we used advanced techniques and taught children many things about learning to read. But my overwhelming conclusion was that most of the children we saw, while they did progress, remained poor readers.

One interpretation of this cataloging of my experiences is that I must be a very bad teacher of reading. I do not teach badly and have had good teaching evaluations. And after doing some research, I have found that other teachers' experiences mirrored my own. For example, in Allington's (1977) *Journal of Reading* article titled "If they don't read much, how they ever gonna get good?" he dared to say,

> To help children who have difficulty developing fluent reading ability, educators have developed remedial and corrective reading classes and a host of training programs, materials, and techniques to use in them. However, even with these intervention processes and strategies, many readers remain poor readers. (p. 57)

He pointed out that poor readers were doing so much skill work that they actually read very little. He followed up this work with investigations that demonstrated differences in instructional practice in high and low reading groups. Reading for high-group readers involved more reading, was focused on meaning, and was infrequently interrupted by the teacher, whereas reading for struggling readers involved little reading, was focused on decoding, and was frequently interrupted by the teacher. In subsequent articles, Allington challenged the rationales and effectiveness of Chapter 1 remedial and special education programs (Walmsley & Allington, 1995). This, of course, comes as no surprise to those who have read *A Nation at Risk* (National Commission on Excellence in Education, 1983), *Becoming a Nation of Readers* (Anderson et al., 1985), and recent U.S. National Assessment of Educational Progress reports (National Center for Educational Statistics, 1995). There is general dissatisfaction with our attempts to teach literacy. The organizational formats we have used for delivering literacy instruction are often woefully inadequate.

I arrived at this conclusion slowly after many years and after my experience in Zimbabwe, where I was a Fulbright Scholar for 15 months in 1985 and 1986. While I was in Zimbabwe, I codirected Project ZIMREAD with Dr. Joyce Childs. The aim of the project was to improve students' reading skills, particularly in English, which was the primary language of instruction (see Roller, 1989, for a full account).

Zimbabwe has several national languages, one of which is English. Most rural children grow up speaking an African language, usually Shona or Ndebele, and are introduced to English when they begin school. They begin reading in English and in their first language early in the first grade. As part of Project ZIMREAD, I taught a third grade demonstration classroom in a rural primary school. I set up my classroom using traditional methods and procedures. I divided the children into three reading groups and instructed them from basal-like, but locally produced, readers. The three-day instructional cycle included a series of activities to be completed before, during, and after the children read their stories. Each group did two seat-work activities and met with me daily. The instruction was considered remarkably successful, particularly for the children in the high group. Within two weeks the children could participate in the small-group lesson and answer questions and summarize the stories in understandable English. They could also perform the seat-work activities independently. When we conducted a demonstration lesson for the faculty of a five-school cluster, we received resounding applause.

Although observers applauded, I was deeply dissatisfied with what we had done. My primary recollection of the experience is of how hard I worked and how little I enjoyed the teaching. I finally realized that it was the "success" itself that was so disturbing. In fact, in a very short time, my Zimbabwean classroom looked very much like the classrooms I was familiar with at home. In both situations, the lessons followed the Initiate-Respond-Evaluate patterns documented in several classroom discourse studies (Barnes, 1976; Bellack et al., 1966; Marshall, Smagorinsky, & Smith, 1995; Mehan, 1979; Wells, 1986). I questioned; they answered; I evaluated. The pattern got us through the lesson and allowed us to achieve our goals—pronouncing vocabulary words, answering questions, and summarizing stories.

But in the Zimbabwean setting, where my students and I were struggling with language barriers (my Shona was about as good as their English; we functioned at about a first grade level in the other's language), I was forced to notice that although we were achieving lesson goals there was no authentic communication going on. I asked the children questions to which I knew the answers, and they knew that I knew the answers. It was this lack of authentic communication in the reading lessons in my Zimbabwe classroom (and, I began to realize, in U.S. classrooms as well) that was at the core of my discontent. Surely, language arts lessons that accommodate the learning of a communication skill without communication do not teach children communication skills. What did these lessons I was teaching have to do with my immersion in the worlds of the novels I love to read? What did they have to do with the skimming and scanning I do of professional reports to find the specific part that will help my understanding?

When I returned to the United States, I found that my own discontent paralleled that in the field and that there were several exciting alternatives to the traditional instructional formats I had been using. Whole language and workshop teaching were acquiring large followings. Both of these movements attracted my attention because they addressed my concern about the artificiality of traditional language lessons. Both movements focus on teaching reading and writing in settings where language is used for authentic purposes. Real communication is a hallmark of the language instruction for both these movements. When I read Hansen (1987), Graves (1983), Wells (1986), and Atwell (1987), the instruction they described did seem related to what I did when I read.

CRITICISMS

Many of the writers I just mentioned offer cogent criticisms of the theories of reading instruction that underlie traditional methods. These theories are usually labeled "bottom-up," "top-down," and "interactive" because they suggest that reading instruction is a complex skill that involves a number of different knowledge sources. Bottom-up theorists view these knowledge sources as those that operate from the bottom, then up (from the print to the head, or brain). Top-down theorists believe the reading process operates from the top, then down (from the head to the print). Interactive theorists believe that the interaction of knowledge sources is complex and not unidirectional. Theorists who lean toward the bottom-up end of the continuum believe that complex behavior is best taught by breaking it into its simpler components and then teaching each one of the components. The assumption is that if students can perform each of the components, they will also be able to perform the complex task. For reading, the simplest components are sounds that go with letters. Bottom-up theorists start there and gradually teach larger and larger units, letter patterns, words, sentences, paragraphs, and whole texts. They believe that reading is primarily a decoding process, the process of translating the letters—marks on the page—into intelligible sounds.

Perhaps the most famous model reflecting this philosophy is the one presented in Gough's 1972 article "One Second of Reading." In this model, the reader begins with the marks on the page and translates them into a phonemic tape, which is forwarded to the librarian, who retrieves the meanings of the words that have been phonemically encoded. The librarian forwards the meanings to Merlin, who uses syntactic and semantic rules to interpret the sentences and then sends the sentences on to TPWSGWTAU, the place where sentences go when they are understood. This information is then forwarded to an editor who uses phonological rules to translate the meanings back into sound, and thus the reader is able to say the words. This bottom-up philosophy underlies the subskills approach to reading that dominated reading series from 1960 until the late 1980s. Four to six major skill areas such as decoding, comprehension, vocabulary, study skills, and literary appreciation, which are divided into a hierarchy of subskills to be taught at various grade levels, were at the heart of these series. Many recent series have abandoned the bottom-up emphasis, but the subskills approach is still present in some.

While there are many bottom-up processes involved in reading, there are cogent criticisms of bottom-up processing as an adequate explanation of how we read. Reading theorists who have proposed schema theory (Anderson & Pearson, 1984) have offered an alternative theory, called top-down. The easiest demonstration of this theory that I have seen is one presented by Rumelhart (1977), who pointed out that the word *event* (handwritten) has different interpretations depending on the context within which it is viewed. For example, if the reader has just read, "Jack had just won the final running _____," the reader will interpret the word as "event." However, if instead the reader has just read, "Jack and Jill _____," the word will most likely be interpreted as the word "went." Rumelhart offered this example as a demonstration of the fact that bottom-up explanations of the reading process are not adequate. They will not explain how an identical word can be interpreted in more than one way.

The arguments about the primacy of bottom-up and top-down processes are largely outdated, and most professionals now agree that reading is an interactive process that involves both bottom-up and top-down processes. However, there is still wide disagreement about which processes are which, which are most important, and how theories of the reading process ought to be related to reading instruction. For instance, many top-down theorists would remain comfortable with the subskills approach to reading instruction. However, they would define skills differently and emphasize top-down rather than bottom-up skills.

I have lost confidence in all these theories to describe learning that results in reading. I suppose this is because of the endless stream of children I have watched learn the short "a" and long "a" patterns, only to come to unknown words that include these sounds and still be unable to say the words. It is also because of the many children I have seen complete endless worksheets on getting the main idea and drawing conclusions who still approach stories without the intent to make sense of them. It is also because of the number of children I have seen who technically *can* read, albeit slowly and haltingly, but refuse to read. All three types of theories seem inadequate to account for the emotional and motivational dimensions of reading difficulties. Many of the children I work with simply hate reading, and they will say quite readily that they hate it. Who wouldn't hate something they have spent years trying to learn and still do not do very well?

There is another set of theorists who find interactive models of reading inadequate because they emphasize thinking processes at the expense of emotional ones. What I believe now is that reading behavior is so complex that the act itself is destroyed when it is broken up into its many small parts. Although children can be taught these parts (sometimes), by the time they learn them they are so removed from the act of reading that they simply do not use what they have learned. The philosophies that underlie whole language and workshop teaching (Goodman, 1986; Graves, 1983; Hansen, 1987; Smith, 1971; Vygotsky, 1978) offer an alternative view of learning to read.

AN ALTERNATIVE

This alternative philosophy is based on theories of early language acquisition. Whole language theorists point out that reading and writing are language activities, and they ask why children who are so easily successful at learning to speak should have difficulty learning to read and write. It is acknowledged that some of the difficulty may relate to differences between oral and written language. But another critical factor may be that children learn to speak and listen in their homes, whereas much other literacy learning occurs in schools.

There are some basic differences in the home and school environments that may account for the difficulties children experience in learning to read and write. The most important difference is that at home early language teaching is done naturally—children learn language in the context of talking about the things they and their parents do together. Thus, parents do not break speech into its logical components, teach their children each one, and give them time to practice. Instead, the child and the parent talk with each other as they go about their daily lives. The parent allows the child to do what the child can do, and when the child cannot do the task the parent takes over. Wells (1986, p. 24) offers this dialogue as an example of how a parent and child collaborate in learning to talk.

33

Mark:	'Ot, Mummy?
Mother:	Hot? Yes, that's the radiator.
Mark:	Been—burn?
Mother:	Burn?
Mark:	Yeh.
Mother:	Yes, you know it'll burn, don't you?
Mark:	(putting hand on radiator) Oh! Ooh!
Mother:	Take your hand off of it.

Notice how the child offers what he is able to say. His mother consistently checks to make sure she is right about what he is trying to say, and then she extends his sentences by putting into words the thoughts he cannot put into words himself.

Activity theory, as it is explained by Russian psychologists such as Leont'ev (1981 as cited in Teale, 1990), bests captures the complex nature of this early language learning as it applies to literacy learning. It acknowledges that as children are learning to read and write, they learn not only how to read and write but also about reading and writing and why they are used. Children must understand all of these in order to understand what it means to become literate. Activity theory, unlike traditional theories, focuses on motives and goals as well as psychological operations such as pattern identification, prediction, and inferencing. Instead of conceptualizing reading as a set of psychological skills and operations that may operate independently of one another, activity theory conceptualizes reading and writing as goal-directed processes. It therefore views the complete activity rather than smaller components as the fundamental unit of learning.

However, a focus on the complete literacy event does not mean that traditional skills, which are listed in the scope and sequences chart of a basal reader, are not important. Rather, these skills are situated within a holistic context that is intimately linked with goals and conditions of reading. Operations are involved, but they are part of the larger activity rather than an accretion of skills. Children internalize whole activities or contexts first. Only as they build their store of literacy experiences, and these experiences resemble one another in some ways and differ in others, do children come to the point where they begin to focus on the psychological operations.

One of the most important aspects of early language learning in the home is that it is frequently based on children's choice. Parents do not teach their children how to talk by deciding what they want their children to talk about and then carefully teaching the vocabulary and grammatical structures that will be necessary to carry on the conversation. Rather, they talk with their children about the topics that come up in the course of daily activities. Wells (1986) reported that more than 60 percent of the time it was children who initiated or chose the topics of conversations he studied.

SPECIFIC CONCERNS ABOUT WORKSHOP TEACHING

As I mentioned, I chose to create a workshop classroom for instruction because it integrated the concept of choice with a holistic approach to learning. I made the decision to have a workshop classroom in our summer program in 1988. How did I make that decision? After all, I was responsible for the educational program of 15 children who were going to spend six weeks of their summer at the clinic. I was also responsible for teaching 28 undergraduate and graduate students how to work with struggling readers. I owed children, parents, and students the best possible experience. Though there were many criticisms of workshop approaches for teaching these children, I was convinced that these criticisms were answerable and that using a workshop method was a reasonable way to teach them.

Several concerns were frequently voiced. Many people emphasized that struggling readers needed an organized structure for lessons if they were to learn. Others wanted to know how I would be able to keep track of the children when they were all reading different materials. Others were concerned about the opportunities for oral reading and teaching comprehension. The most frequently voiced concern was about skills: people said things such as, "Well, it might work for the good kids, but you need to teach the poor readers the skills." Related to this issue, many questioned how we would use direct instruction as well. Following, I will explain more about the reasons for these concerns and about my answers to criticism of the workshop classroom.

Structure

The concerns about structure arose because there is an apparent lack of organization in workshop classrooms. Many U.S. classrooms use basal readers and ability grouping for reading instruction. Others use some form of literature-based instruction that involves children reading books the teacher has selected or children choosing from a set of four or five teacher-selected books. In these classrooms, instruction is organized around reading groups, as mentioned earlier. Teachers in these classrooms usually set aside a block of time for reading instruction and have their groups rotate among three activities: (1) meeting with the teacher, (2) completing seat work in accompanying workbooks and ditto sheets or, in the case of literature-based instruction, some sort of creative project, and (3) working in centers where the teacher may encourage extension and enrichment activities. Observers who walk into these classrooms during reading time see the teacher meeting with a group of children. Usually the teacher is leading a discussion about the story in a reader or the assigned trade book, explaining how to do assigned workbook pages or dittos, reviewing a particularly troublesome workbook page or ditto, or explaining how to do a project associated with a book. There are some children at their desks reading silently or doing projects, workbooks, or dittos, and sometimes there are smaller groups of children at various places in the room engaged in some sort of center activity.

Observers who walk into a workshop classroom during reading or writing workshop time may see no organization in what is happening. They see children scattered around the room talking and reading, and they do not recognize familiar patterns. However, workshop classrooms are as highly structured as the traditional classrooms just described. Whereas traditional classrooms are organized around the three types of activities mentioned, the workshop format is similarly organized around a restricted set of activities. It has a basic three-part structure, group-read-group or group-write-group, as explained in Chapter Two. The first group session is devoted to direct instruction. During the reading or writing time, three or four acceptable activities may occur as the teacher holds individual conferences with children. The second group period is devoted to group sharing. Once observers are aware of this pattern, the structure of the workshop classroom becomes more visible.

Materials

Another obvious contrast between the two types of classrooms is the instructional materials used. Although there often are some basal readers in workshop classrooms and some of the children choose to use them occasionally, trade books are overwhelmingly the materials in use. Most of the time there are as many different books being read as there are children reading. This is most confusing to observers. How can a classroom be orderly and well organized if all the children are reading different materials? The answer to this question is that the activities in basal readers and many literature-based classrooms are dependent on materials and the teacher. In workshop classrooms the activities are more child based rather than materials or teacher based. Reading silently, partner reading, preparing to read to a younger child, writing a response to reading, writing a draft, revising, editing, and sharing are all activities that can be done independently with any text or topic. Initially, the teacher's responsibility is to teach the children how to do the activities. Once an activity has been taught, the children can do it with minimal supervision. Because the activities are designed to work with a wide range of materials, having the children read different books is not a problem.

Oral Reading

Another part of traditional reading instruction that observers often do not see in workshop classrooms is oral reading. Children in workshop classrooms do not sit in a circle and take turns reading. This is a bad practice in any classroom but nonetheless is typically associated with basal reading instruction, particularly for the low reading groups (Allington, 1983). However, different types of oral reading do occur in workshop classrooms. Children often read to one another during the reading workshop time because they want to share their stories. They sometimes read a favorite part of their books during sharing time. They may read aloud to younger children. Sometimes the teacher will ask the children to read aloud for diagnostic reasons, particularly when the teacher is checking the appropriateness of the children's book choices. Children's oral reading is an important part of workshop classrooms. It simply occurs in settings unfamiliar to observers. The important guideline that governs oral reading in any classroom is that its purpose should be authentic.

Comprehension

Observers also wonder where the comprehension discussions are in workshop classrooms. They are accustomed to seeing the teacher, often armed with questions prepared by the basal authors, conducting a gentle inquisition with a small group of children. The teacher asks a question, a child answers, then the teacher evaluates and moves on to the next question. In this setting we traditionally thought we were teaching comprehension, although we have acknowledged since at least 1978 (Durkin, 1978–79) that most of what occurs in these sessions is not instruction but assessment.

There are many activities in workshop classrooms during which children learn comprehension skills. They learn to comprehend during reading time when they are trying to construct meaning from the books they have chosen. Understanding and responding to a story are major focuses of individual conferences with children. During oral literature there is a lot of questioning and talk about the story. Both my talk and the children's talk make internal comprehension processes audible. The talk verbalizes the thinking that underlies good comprehension. But perhaps the time period most analogous to the traditional small-group discussion is sharing time. During sharing children both practice and develop their comprehension strategies.

My own responses to sharing convinced me of its importance. I enjoy talking to someone who has just finished reading a book that I have recently read or one that I love. I look forward to telling what I liked, how I responded, what I didn't like, which character I thought was terrible, which character I admired, and which one reminded me of myself or someone else I know. I enjoy hearing what someone else thinks or feels about the same book. Sometimes I discover through others what I had not discovered myself. For example, I shared the book *Nervous Conditions* by Tsitsi Dangarembga with a group of women. Someone who had not read it asked why I thought the main character was able to reject her father's definition of women's roles. Was it because she had been exposed to another culture? I didn't know the answer. It made me revisit the book and find out that exposure to another culture was very important in explaining how the child was able to reject her father's definition. The act of sharing reminds me of the satisfaction reading and writing bring and makes me continue reading and writing. The connections between sharing, understanding, and motivation make sharing essential to the workshop.

A careful analysis of the dialogue about sunken treasure ships in Chapter Two will show that the children's talk was aimed at making sense of the sunken ship story. By working together, they established that the search for the sunken treasure had taken a long time. They did this as they talked with one another and used such skills as revisiting the text and drawing inferences to answer questions that they had raised.

Skills

Perhaps the biggest concern of workshop classroom observers is skills teaching. How can children be taught to read if there is no systematic teaching of skills? If teachers do not follow a scope and sequence chart such as those typically provided by basal series, how can they be sure that all the children are learning what they need to be learning? It is at this point that the philosophies of the two types of classrooms are most divergent. In a traditional classroom it is assumed that the act of reading can be broken down into a set of discrete skills that can be taught in sequence. Children are thought to become readers by mastering this sequence of skills.

Proponents of whole language and workshop instruction challenge this assumption. They believe that reading is so complex that it cannot be broken down into a set of subskills that, when taught, will assure that children will learn to read. They believe that the division of reading into skills is arbitrary and that even if it were not arbitrary there would be too many skills to teach directly. They also believe that reading environments (books, purposes, and participants) are fairly unique and that each situation may call for unique combinations of skills. Therefore, the better approach is to put children in situations where they are actually reading and writing and to address the particular skills needed in particular situations as they occur. If classrooms provide extended opportunities for reading, the skills that need to be taught can be addressed.

Teachers in the workshop setting substitute observation and careful analysis of children's performance in particular literacy situations for scope and sequence charts. For example, in Chapter Two I noted that my observations and notes from the first week suggested that book choice, using meaning cues for word identification, and substituting letters to pronounce proper names would be appropriate skills for many children to learn next. As a teacher in a workshop classroom observes children in the whole group and independent settings, he or she watches what the children are actually doing and then works with the children on the particular skills that need to be addressed at that particular time. This is possible because the focus of teaching in workshop classrooms has shifted away from reading materials and content toward the individual child. The teacher does not need to spend a lot of time planning a series of questions to use with a particular selection. He or she does not need to create supplementary worksheets to go with the story nor spend a lot of time creating activities for centers. The day-to-day operation of the workshop classroom is dependent on a set of activities that always stay the same. For example, the teacher does not need to plan reading sharing. All the children know how to do reading sharing and know that they are to be prepared for it.

When teachers' time is released from planning daily activities, their attention and time is free for focusing on specific children. They can keep detailed records of children's learning. Workshop teachers spend their planning time focusing on specific children selected for conferences the next day. They review the children's work, look at the goals children have set for themselves, and think about what kinds of information they want to gather about them or what kinds of skills they might want to work on in a daily conference.

Direct Instruction

Another aspect of skills instruction that often disturbs visitors in a workshop classroom is that they do not often see teachers doing anything that resembles what they think of as teaching. For the most part, workshop teachers take this traditional role only briefly. Some teachers do direct teaching during short minilessons; other teachers do most of the direct instruction during oral literature as they read to children; and others do a lot of direct teaching in individual and small-group conferences. A minilesson often includes what would constitute the introduction, instruction, and modeling steps of the traditional direct-instruction lesson. However, the guided practice, independent practice, and evaluation steps for the instruction are carried on in the independent setting. Workshop teachers do not produce a series of worksheets or a set of specified tasks that they designate for guided practice, independent practice, and evaluation. Instead, they keep the specific individual and group goals in mind and then meet with the children, either individually or in a small group, to follow up the minilessons as it is appropriate.

When I talk to teachers who have read about workshop and whole language classrooms, they often think that direct instruction should not be included in their classroom. They associate direct instruction with traditional classrooms and think that instruction is incidental in workshop classrooms. This is a dangerous misconception. Direct instruction occurs in all good classrooms. In workshop classrooms it is often associated with selecting a book, responding to a book, sharing a book, as well as with specific skills such as using quotation marks or summarizing the story. There is direct instruction in good workshop classrooms; it is simply located in different places and sometimes devoted to different content than in traditional classrooms. For example, one of the most basic skills readers must have in order to be independent readers and learners is the skill of choosing a book. I teach that skill in a minilesson, reviewing the characteristics of easy or vacation (independent level) books, just right (instructional level) books, and dream (frustration level) books. In my individual conferences I have children read from the books they have selected, ask what type of book they think it is, and if necessary work with a child until I am sure that he or she can select an appropriate book. During sharing time the children will often reinforce this lesson, casually indicating what kind of book they are sharing.

When I am talking with teachers in inservice settings about direct teaching of skills, it is at about this time that one of the teachers will say, "Get serious. When I say skills I don't mean choosing a book! What about short 'a'?" Well, what about short "a"? There is no reason that short "a" cannot be taught in a minilesson and reinforced during conferences and sharing time. If a particular child or children need to learn short "a," then it should be taught. The children I teach in the summer have already been exposed to many hours of short "a" instruction. They usually know short "a," but they are much less likely to be able to use context in figuring out unknown words. So, I am more likely to teach the latter. In first grade classrooms using a workshop approach, I often see minilessons taught about initial consonant sounds, usually delivered in the context of reading a predictable book that uses the particular sound frequently. The point is that the skills taught should depend on the children being taught.

IN SCHOOL CLASSROOMS

I believe the workshop structure is the best approach for literacy instruction for all students. The structure of a workshop classroom allows real reading and writing to occur. The group-read-group or group-write-group structure allows for both direct instruction and independent reading, and it provides an atmosphere where children can experience the activity and begin to understand the whys and what fors of reading and writing. I believe that if children understand this, the probability that they will learn the hows of reading is greatly enhanced.

This is particularly important for the children who are having difficulty learning to read. These are the children who have been skilled and drilled into sounding-out machines, as are many of the children I encounter in SRP. Often their only response when they come to a word they do not know is to groan until someone tells them the word. Time after time I have encountered children who think of reading as little more than getting to the end of a line without a mistake. They hate reading. I think this hatred is largely the result of viewing reading as sounding out words. They do not understand that reading is a passport into fantastic worlds and a door to incredible amounts of information. It is perhaps most important that these children experience real reading, and it is the challenge of a workshop to provide those experiences.

I do not want to leave the impression that I believe children having difficulty with reading should be separated from their peers and provided with a workshop setting. Rather, I believe that a workshop setting is the best setting for *all* children to learn to read. Both students who are having difficulty reading and students who are more advanced in their reading abilities can function within the structure of a single workshop classroom. The fact that workshops allow teachers to focus on individual children means that workshop classrooms can be productive settings for all children. This book focuses on diversity in reading ability because that is the primary type of diversity contained in the summer reading program I teach. But the workshop setting is also a positive structure for dealing with cultural, ethnic, racial, and socioeconomic diversity. The fact that my classroom includes mostly struggling readers is an artifact of the situation. There is still considerable variability in reading levels, and the variability in chronological ages is considerably greater than that of most classrooms. Workshop classrooms are unique in their ability to provide for a wide range of individual differences while using organizational structures that treat all children equally.

Chapter Four

Choice Makes Reading Instruction Child Centered

with Linda G. Fielding

TO SUCCEED in a reading workshop children must choose books they both want to read and can read. Learning to choose good books is one of the goals of the SRP classroom. Most children do this most of time, but there are children who struggle with choice. They choose books and reading materials that they either do not want to read, cannot read, or both. At first, this may seem outrageous. Why would children choose either a book that they don't want to read or one that they can't read? And yet they do.

For some children book choice, or difficulty level of reading material, is associated with social status. Reading is very much a factor in children's construction of their roles in the classroom. Even though many classrooms have abandoned ability grouping, what children read is part of who they are. First grade children proudly announce that they are reading chapter books and their classmates who cannot may envy them and feel quite distraught about their own inability. Children do not want to be marked as inferior by the books they read. When Karen first came to SRP she spent several days paging through a book that I was certain she could not read. She would turn periodically to whomever would listen and announce what page she was on. She turned every single page and spent an appropriate amount of time looking at each one. There were a few pictures in the book, and when I stopped to talk with her about the book, she told me about the pictures. Karen had experienced years of reading failure. She desperately wanted to convince the people in this new setting that she was a good reader.

Whereas status is a major concern for some children, for others choice is constrained by interests—both their own and those of their peers. Many struggling readers are simply not interested in the topics and content of the materials they can read with acceptable accuracy. As struggling readers get older, this problem grows even worse because most easy books are designed for the interests of younger children. Here are the voices of two children as they talk about easy books.

> Heidi: I don't like to read easy books. They're BAAABY books and they're BOORRRING.
>
> Mark: Easy books. EEEasy books. They're all so boring. All so boring. I don't like to read easy book. I think the reason why you read is to...hear interesting stories. I don't like reading easy books. Don't usually have much in them. (Forbes & Roller, 1991, pp. 5–6)

In addition, as children grow older the pressure to conform to their peers' interests grows. Finders (1994) reported that a young girl she studied who read a wide range of materials, including many books and articles about sports, never read or talked about sports books in class. Apparently, she felt that sports books were inappropriate for girls. Lewis (1995) in her study of a fifth and sixth grade classroom found that there was a great deal of peer pressure among the girls to read books by Christopher Pike and R.L. Stine. The popular children passed these around and talked with one another about them at recess. At one independent reading time she noticed that almost every girl was reading one of these two authors. Similarly, an adult who had read Nancy Drew books as a child reported that she had actually liked the Trixie Belden books better, but she read Nancy Drew because that is what the girls in her class passed around (Gonzalez, 1994). Children do not want to be marked as different by the books they read. Books are a way children can identify with their peers.

MAKING CHOICE POSSIBLE

While each year some children at SRP have trouble with choice, others are successful. Choice launches them into the world of readers. Wells's book *The Meaning Makers* (1986) helped me understand why choice is so important. His studies point out that early language learning occurring in the home is guided by and responsive to the child, whereas literacy learning in school contexts is directed by teachers and is less responsive. At home the children he studied chose 64 percent of the topics of conversation, whereas at school the children chose only 23 percent of the topics (p. 68). Wells suggested that early language learning is highly successful because children pursue their own topics a majority of the time. They talk about topics *they* choose, topics they *want* to talk about. Parents and caregivers tend to follow children's lead, which allows a great deal of language learning to occur. Other research shows that at home children choose their own reading material as well (Phillips & McNaughton, 1990).

The type of learning that occurs at home capitalizes on intrinsic motivation—motivation that comes from inside the child. When children are intrinsically motivated they learn because they *want* to do what they are doing. As children are doing something they enjoy and following their interests, they learn language. Researchers report that intrinsic motivation frequently produces higher levels of sustained interest and better learning (Malone & Lepper, 1987). Including choice in instructional environments takes advantage of the interest and learning benefits of intrinsic motivation. When children choose their own reading materials, they are more likely to read texts that tell them something they want to know. If they want to know, they will persist in their struggle to construct meaning. The struggle for meaning provides the motivation for learning and practicing reading. In my classroom, book choice serves two functions: first, it takes advantage of intrinsic motivation, and second, it breaks a lock-step system that has all children reading the same text when it is impossible to choose a single text that is appropriate for all.

Choice is only as wide as the alternatives available. For children to choose books that they *can* read, the difficulty range of books in any classroom must be very wide. Sixth grade, and even high school classrooms, must include easy picture books, and first grade classrooms must include age- and interest-appropriate novels. Often classroom libraries contain a rather narrow range of books deemed appropriate for the average child of that grade. We do this despite our knowledge of the variability in reading capabilities and interests of the children in any particular grade. Our selections for classroom and school libraries must acknowledge the range of reading abilities that exist in every classroom.

In addition, the range of types of materials available is important. Some children love stories; others hate to read them because they are not true. Some children like nature books; others like books about machinery. Some children look through the books in their classrooms only to find that there are none about children like them. Classrooms must have many books and other print materials available—newsprint, catalogs, advertisements, classroom announcements, directions, poetry, nonfiction, story books, and so on. And these must include materials on a wide array of topics, in many genres, from a numerous variety of cultures and life settings. The range must be as wide as possible so that as many children as possible can find books they both want to and can read.

However, the problem of choice is not as simple as providing a wide and appropriate range of reading materials. This is only the first step. Teachers must also create a classroom atmosphere that encourages real choice. If children are to have real choice, one of the first tasks is to create an environment that encourages differences. The children's prejudices against easy books are deeply held. To get struggling readers reading, teachers must first find ways to enable them to read some of the books they want to read, and then find ways to make them want to read the books they can read. Teachers, in short, must "make difficult books accessible and easy books acceptable" (Forbes & Roller, 1991, p. 7). Linda Fielding, who is the SRP classroom teacher in alternate years, and I have had students who struggle with choice every summer. We have written about some strategies for encouraging real choice in an article published in *The Reading Teacher* (1992). Much of that article is reproduced here.

KNOWING WHEN A BOOK IS JUST RIGHT

Some children really do not know how to find a book they are able to read. Erin, a fourth grade girl in the SRP classroom, was a good example. She could not find a book she could read because she did not have a clear conception of what it meant to be able to read a book. She was very excited about reading a chapter book. During a book conference, though, I discovered that while Erin could talk about a few incidents in the chapters, she had no sense of the story. From her reading log, I realized she was reading the chapters out of sequence. Erin thought reading random chapters was appropriate. Although the book was not making much sense, nothing Erin read made much sense to her. She was accustomed to reading material from basal anthologies that were too difficult for her. Random chapters from her book made as much sense to Erin as the selections from readers had made. She conceptualized reading as plowing through brief selections.

The difficulties that struggling readers have in monitoring their own reading are well documented (for example, see Baker & Brown, 1984). In workshop classrooms an important self-monitoring goal for children is being able to select books that are of appropriate difficulty. In the SRP classroom I spend a good deal of time teaching children how to select books. In an article entitled "Lesson from Goldilocks: 'Somebody's Been Choosing My Books But I Can Make My Own Choices Now!'" Ohlhausen and Jepsen (1992) present a method for helping children learn to select books. They recommend a direct instruction process that begins with teacher modeling and moves through guided practice to independent performance. They teach children to label books as "too easy," "just right," and "too hard"—designations that correspond roughly to the independent, instructional, and frustration levels traditionally associated with informal reading inventories. In SRP, I teach children to judge book difficulty based on such factors as word and concept difficulty, fluency of oral reading, and how much help is needed to read the book. Ohlhausen and Jepsen's questions (1992, p. 36) are helpful to children in making these decisions. For example, to find a "just right" book they suggest asking the following:

1. Is this book new to you?
2. Do you understand some of the book?
3. Are there just a few words per page you don't know?
4. When you read are some places smooth and some choppy?
5. Can someone help you with the book? Who?

MAKING DIFFICULT BOOKS ACCESSIBLE

Children deserve access to interesting content even when their reading abilities do not match the demands of the texts containing that content. Such access is important because without it struggling readers will develop knowledge deficits. In addition, they may be excluded from many important events of classroom life when they cannot read the texts that are the basis of those events. In the following sections we describe several ways to make difficult books accessible.

Allowing Independent Reading Time

When children choose books that are too difficult for them, they should be allowed to spend some independent time with them. They often can have positive interactions around difficult books. Although the children cannot read these books, a group of them can often interact enough to discover what they want to know, and when they cannot they often ask for help. From such interactions with difficult books children can gain increased content knowledge, which may make future reading tasks easier. Children may also learn a lot about the reading process from the conversations that surround their struggles with these books.

Hunt (1970) argued that children learn something from books that they have selected themselves, out of interest, even if their oral reading accuracy rating on those books falls well outside the generally accepted 95 percent cutoff. Certainly Susan, an SRP student mentioned earlier, learned a lot from the three or four class periods she spent with several books about sharks that were well beyond her capabilities. The following is a typescript reproduction of an early draft of her own shark book:

> Shark's are very dangerous. a shark can't get your arm when a men is protcked by armor. Sharks onwle live in satwater. The shark can et her onw baby. The mother can put her baby in her moth. The Great White Shark eats 300lbs of met ever day. Sharks are faster at swmi than peolp. Shars have strong jaws. The Great White Shark is 14 fl long. And they weighing is around 700 kg to (1540 lb).

Reading to Children

Another way to give children access to difficult books is to read to the children from them. Struggling readers need to be exposed to the possibilities that books offer. Often when children's reading abilities fall behind their peers', their knowledge and vocabulary size also fall behind because there is so much book knowledge that they cannot access. Adult reading is critical in this situation. In fact, Susan originally became enthralled with sharks when I read to her class from a large, expensive, and difficult book about sharks. Reading to children constantly reminds them that reading is the passport to marvelous stories and fascinating stores of information.

Partner Reading

Partner reading is another activity that allows children to read beyond their accuracy levels. In a second grade workshop classroom, Linda saw struggling and capable readers frequently pair themselves. They engaged in a sophisticated version of what has been termed "shared reading" (Copperman, 1986)—when an adult reads a text in a way that allows the child to chime in and take over on the parts he or she can handle. In the SRP classroom, the more able reader often served as the "adult" and the less able reader as the "child."

Rereading

Rereading also is a practice that helps make hard books accessible. There is evidence, much of it from studies of older struggling readers (Herman, 1985; Samuels, 1979), that when children read passages repeatedly, not only do these passages become easier, but also children are able to read new passages at about the same difficulty level more fluently. Erin talked about this after sharing *The Z Was Zapped* by Chris Van Allsburg with her classmates. One of them asked, "How did you know all the words in that book?" Erin explained that originally the book had been a dream book (too difficult) for her, but Dr. Roller read it to her. Then she read it many times and the book was now a just right book for her. Sometimes we substitute a tape recording of the book for a live reading to provide the initial fluent model for children to listen to one or more times before they practice the book themselves.

Preceding Difficult Books with Easier Books

Teachers can also decrease the difficulty of harder books by preceding them with easier books on the same topic or theme. In nonfiction reading, the easier book can serve to remind children of what they already know and give them a chance to encounter in print some technical words about the topic. Then, they are primed to read the harder book. This is a version of activating or building background knowledge. Atwell (1987) suggests a similar procedure for writing reports. I recently watched a tutor apply the same concept with fiction reading. Because her student liked scary books, she helped him read easier scary books to build a web of words he was likely to encounter in harder ones. This gave him the background and confidence to attempt some of the harder books and to be successful with them.

Another student, Matt, experienced the same effect during his independent reading of *Baseball's Heavy Hitters* by Angelo G. Resciniti. Each chapter describes the career of a different baseball star, but the chapter organization, vocabulary (words such as "league" and "championship"), and style of language (the word "a tape-measure homerun" for example) remain similar throughout. Although Matt was highly motivated to read the book, it was at or close to his frustration level when he began reading it, and he was encouraged to balance the time he spent on that book with time on books that were less difficult for him. As he progressed through the book, however, the structures and words that had been difficult at first became familiar to him. As Matt put it, "It was hard in the first chapter, but when I got to the last chapters it was easier because I knew the words."

There are a number of ways to make difficult but enticing books more accessible. These practices honor children's choices and interests and give them access to vocabulary and content knowledge that will make future reading easier for them.

MAKING EASY BOOKS ACCEPTABLE

It is equally important to dignify children's reading of books that are appropriate for them in difficulty but contain subject matter intended for a younger audience. Noncompetitive, nonability-grouped classrooms in which children regularly self-select books of various difficulty levels can do much to remove the stigma of reading easy books. Beyond providing that type of classroom, there are other steps teachers can take.

Modeling Use and Enjoyment of Easy Books

When Linda and I model our own use and enjoyment of easy books, it has helped legitimize easy books in our classrooms. We tell the children that in our own adult lives, most of the pleasure reading we do is easy. We also show our appreciation of the very easiest books for children. In the summer classroom, for example, we have shared lots of patterned books to model how much we like their pattern, rhythm, and repetition. One time I chanted *King Bidgood's in the Bathtub* by Audrey Wood and *Cats and Kittens* authored and published by Scott, Foresman—both patterned books—and explained why I like them. Peter, a fifth grade child, then shared the book *Mrs. Wishy Washy* by Joy Cowley with the class. He began the session, "I like this book 'cause it goes like 'The King's in the bathtub and he won't get out.' It's actually the same thing but it's a little bit funnier" (Forbes & Roller, 1991, p. 7).

Altering Purposes for Easy Reading

Another way to legitimize easy reading is to alter its purposes. For example, while easy reading is often done because it is enjoyable, many struggling readers see easy reading as necessary practice. However, if they read easy books to a younger audience, reading these books has a legitimate purpose. The struggling readers can improve their own abilities in a setting that is enjoyable for everyone involved (Ford & Ohlhausen, 1988; Labbo & Teale, 1990). Classrooms that have a program of older children reading to younger children make easy books acceptable and show that they belong in the hands of every reader. With struggling readers it is important that the age difference between reader and listener is sizable and that the pairings are arranged carefully so that the older struggling reader is not paired with a younger child who reads better than he or she does.

In the SRP classroom, we have a program of reading to children at a nearby daycare center. All the readers in our classroom then have legitimate purposes for reading easy books. As they prepare to read books to younger children, the older children receive the repeated practice that enables them to develop fluency. And as they consider whether and how to share various books with their young partners, they think critically about the content, structure, and themes of the books. Eleven-year-old Millie, for example, decided that *Lazy Mary* by June Melser would be perfect for young children because of its repetition, rhyme, and humor. But she decided against one of her favorite books, *My Puppy Is Born* by Joanna Cole, because she felt that the photographs of the puppies' birth were more suitable for older children.

Taping Books

Another motivator for reading easy books is the tape recorder. Originally we thought that we would use the tape recorder to record difficult stories for children's listening. However, the children in our classroom thought differently. They wanted to make tapes for others to listen to. Because they wanted to sound good on tape, they chose easy books to read. Of course, choosing easy books and practicing them for tape recording also gave the children the opportunity to read fluently, which is an important reading goal (Allington, 1983).

Challenging Preconceptions About Easy Books

Dignifying children's reading of easy books can also be achieved by challenging children's notions that easy books are boring. Picture books appeal to children and adults of all ages and levels of sophistication. They can easily be a part of the literacy selections in upper grade as well as primary classrooms. Some easy books have very sophisticated plots that mirror the intricate plots of TV shows, movies, and harder books. Sometimes it is not the words of a story but rather the plot, concepts, and characters that determine whether it is interesting or boring. Simple words, such as those in the folktale "The Three Billy Goats Gruff," may belie the complex story they convey.

Book sharing sessions help make this point. The summer classroom discussion about *Mrs. Wishy Washy*, a portion of which is excerpted and discussed following, offers a convincing argument that all stories have more to them than just their words. Peter, the student leading the discussion, read the book to the children. There was considerable interaction as these 8- to 12-year olds anticipated the ending. In the subsequent conversation, the children and I discussed the ending and talked about why Peter liked the book. Jason introduced the topic of keeping animals clean by saying, "Well, you can't really keep farm

51

animals clean because they go back in the mud on the farm." A lively discussion followed.

> Peter: Um.
> Roller: I think that's what makes this story funny, 'cause Mrs. Wishy Washy works so hard at something that's...
> Child: Just isn't going work.
> Child: Something that...
> Jimmy: And then they go right back in the mud and she probably has to drag 'em back out, and then they run away and get 'em again, and they run away.

After a brief diversion to another topic Peter began again.

> Peter: You know, I know one way to keep cows clean. Put 'em in a clean field.
> Child: Huh?
> Peter: Put 'em in a, um...
> Holly: No, I have a way. She'd just put, like sidewalks, no mud around it or anything.

After an interruption Holly continued.

> Holly: And then, and then put a gate around it.
> Mary: A giant gate.
> Holly: And you take, it won't get into mud and then they'll be really clean.

Who would have anticipated that *Mrs. Wishy Washy* could spark such an enthusiastic discussion among third through sixth grade children? This story and many others that older children have sometimes sneered at are fascinating, fun, and entertaining. When sharing becomes a regular part of the reading class, all children can get involved in discussions of easier books. When struggling readers hear capable readers enjoying a discussion of easy books, the stigma of reading these books begins to disappear.

Broadening the Concept of Acceptable Reading

Often the books that are easy enough for struggling older readers are not about topics that are interesting to an older child. Our suggestion is to alleviate this problem by broadening the concept of what counts as acceptable reading material. Materials that are interesting to older readers sometimes have the same predictable, repetitive features found in the best material for younger, beginning readers. They also include literary forms or genres used far too infrequently—poems, songs, raps, cheers, jump-rope chants, and children's own writing and dictations. For example, Joanna Cole collected a number of popular jump-rope chants in *Anna Banana*; and with Stephanie Calmenson she assembled children's street rhymes in *Miss Mary Mack and Other Children's Street Rhymes*. We have a tendency to limit reading materials to books, but offering the types of materials just mentioned would provide older readers with reading that is interesting and at an appropriate difficulty level.

Making Nonfiction Available

We cannot emphasize strongly enough the importance of making nonfiction more available and more familiar to students. Much of what we know about science and some of the more interesting things we know about history we have learned from simple children's books. We need to share this with children and read nonfiction to them on a regular basis. We should guard against children's perceptions that books are "too easy" or "boring" just because many of the words are easy for them. If the books contain new concepts, they are worth reading. For example, 12-year-old Jamie, a student in the SRP classroom, was delighted to find David Drew's *Tadpole Diary*. As Jamie explained to the class,

> I live by a lake and I have tadpoles out there. And I go down every day during the summer and catch them. So I found this book here, and I started to read it.

From this book Jamie learned when milestones in the cycle from egg to tadpole to frog occur, and he had the satisfaction of being able to figure out challenging words such as "magnifying glass" and "camouflage" because of the supportive context in which they occurred.

THE CHILDREN'S VIEWS

Linda and I have found that the activities described in this chapter do help struggling readers read more successfully the somewhat difficult books they want to read. These activities also help readers make the transition from selecting inappropriately to choosing books that are appropriate for them. The voices of children themselves provide the most compelling argument for bringing struggling readers together with books in ways that ensure success.

The following discussion in the summer classroom reveals what happens when children are pressed to read teacher-selected books that are too difficult. Linda Fielding had asked, "What could teachers do that would help you get more interested in reading and like reading more?"

Carrie:	You could tell them to start from easy books and then when you know everything you can read harder books.
Josh:	That's what I was going to say.
Fielding:	Can you say a little more about that?
Carrie:	Well, see, when you know the words and you've seen it a whole bunch of times in all these easy books, um, that when you get a little bit harder books that you understand a little bit more better...without missing a whole bunch of those words.
Fielding:	At school, do you have reading and writing set up this way so that you pick books that you want to read and topics that you want to write about?
Matt:	Not for reading.
Rob:	Sometimes.
Matt:	Sometimes. Sometimes the teacher'll pick a mystery book that you have to read or something.
Carrie:	If you don't know how to read that book, it's like you get way behind.
Fielding:	Does that happen sometimes? Do you get into...
Carrie:	Yeah.
Matt:	I got way ahead.
Rob:	Then you're on Chapter 2 and then you got to read to Chapter 5 or something. Got to take it home every night.
Carrie:	You're so embarrassed that you don't want to read the book any longer.
Fielding:	Is that because the book is a little bit too hard?
Carrie:	Sometimes, then you're like slowing down and the class is way ahead.

In contrast, Mark, another child from the summer reading classroom, is a good example of a student who knows how and is encouraged to select materials he can read. In SRP, he and his peers were encouraged to spend most of their time with easy (independent level) books. When he returned to his third grade classroom the following fall, he felt confident in his choice of books. He explained to a group of friends,

> I know these books are really easy for you, but I need to read them because I have a lot of trouble reading. If I keep practicing my reading with these books, I'll get better.

In School Classrooms

All these suggestions are intended for implementation in school classrooms. The acceptance of difference in classrooms is critical to struggling readers' development. These suggestions work most of the time with most of the children at SRP. However, the challenge of difference in school classrooms is even more marked. Although school classrooms have fewer struggling readers than the SRP classroom, they usually have children whose reading abilities vary more widely. This wider range means that the potential for discriminating against children on the basis of their reading ability is greater. However, workshop classrooms *can* meet this challenge. When Mark told his classmates that reading easy books helped him, he was in a workshop classroom.

The most important thing for school classroom teachers to do is to set a positive expectation for difference. In SRP, the morning group talk time is the place where we do much of this work. When talking with the children we try to emphasize our values—variation in reading ability is normal and to be expected, all the children can learn to read if they are allowed to progress at their own pace, and we are a helping class. We tell them repeatedly that helping impresses us, and we ask the children about who has helped whom. We are honest and open with children about differences, and we are careful to respond as positively to children who read and share easy books as we are to those who read more difficult texts. It is reading appropriate level text that we reinforce. We do not tolerate ridicule in any form; if we hear a whisper of it, we immediately, openly, and loudly squelch it. We do not make fun of anyone else's reading ability in our room or anywhere.

In school classrooms, the challenge goes beyond accepting differences in reading ability to accepting cultural, ethnic, racial, and socioeconomic diversity as well. The ability of teachers to focus on individual children in workshop settings is a major mechanism for encouraging and building on diversity. While accepting difference is a challenge, we must succeed. Our success or failure will determine whether some children learn to read.

Chapter Five

Sharing Gives Children the Lead

with Penny L. Beed

S HARING IS the heart of the workshop day and a crucial mechanism for dealing with individual differences. It is one of the activities that focus on the fourth classroom goal, "Make reading make sense." In Chapter Three, I talked about how teachers' planning time is used differently in workshop classrooms. In my classroom I am not constantly planning activities, writing sets of questions, and making worksheets. Instead, I use my planning time to focus on a few children and think about what each child has been doing recently, what each child might need help with, and some possibilities for what each child might do next. Instead of directing activities, I interact with children and respond to what they are doing. When they need help to accomplish what they have set out to do, I offer help by "leading from behind," which I mentioned earlier.

In most traditional classrooms, teachers lead from the front: the talk from the front of the classroom is content and skills oriented and teacher centered. The teacher centeredness means that much of children's uniqueness is overlooked. Leading from behind requires me to use a different style of language, and sharing is one of the places that this change in role is most apparent. Rather than expecting all children to follow my thoughts, leading from behind makes me follow children's thoughts. In doing so, the children are released from the strictures of canonical interpretations and freed to express their own, sometimes quite variable ones. The children's talk during sharing in our workshop classroom is very different from the talk in traditional literature discussions. For one thing, there is a lot more of it; for another, it is often about topics I would

56

never have thought about introducing. Because the talk is more child centered, it gives more space for variability.

TRADITIONAL DISCUSSION FORMATS

To compare the book discussion talk in a traditional classroom with that in a workshop classroom, I have created a hypothetical, traditional discussion about a book called *Have You Seen the Crocodile?* by Colin West. It is a patterned book, which begins with a parrot asking, "Have you seen the crocodile? 'No,' said the dragonfly." The next page continues, "'Have you seen the crocodile?' asked the parrot and the dragonfly. 'No,' said the bumblebee." The pattern builds until six animals conclude, "No one's seen the crocodile!" The next page reads, "'I'VE SEEN THE CROCODILE!' snapped the crocodile. 'But, has anyone seen the parrot, and the dragonfly, and the bumblebee, and the butterfly, and the hummingbird, and the frog?' asked the crocodile." The pictures are quite suggestive. On the last pages the crocodile is licking its lips. A traditional classroom discussion of this book might go something like this.

Teacher: MMmm. Why do the other animals want to know where the crocodile is? James?

James: Maybe he's the leader?

Teacher: Well...maybe. Sharon?

Sharon: Because they want to see him?

Teacher: Why would they want to see him? What do you know about crocodiles? Tom, what do you know about crocodiles?

Tom: They live in Africa.

Teacher: Right! They do live in Africa. What else do you know about crocodiles, Tom?

Tom: Well, they have pointed jaws, no they have square jaws. Oh, I can't remember which is which between crocodiles and alligators!

Teacher: I think crocodiles are pointed, but I'm not absolutely sure. We could look that up. But the jaw certainly is an important part of an alligator, isn't it? Why would I say that, Jane?

Jane: Because crocodiles are vicious. They eat all kinds of other animals.

Teacher: That's right, Jane! Crocodiles are vicious! So, why do you think the other animals want to know where the crocodile is? James?

James: Because the crocodile is dangerous?

Teacher: That's right! The crocodile is dangerous and so they want to know where it is because...

James: They don't want the crocodile to catch them!

Teacher:	Right, James! Good thinking! Now, here at the end, the crocodile is asking, "Have you seen the parrot, the bumblebee, the dragonfly?" Why is the crocodile asking about the other animals?
Sharon:	Because he wants to know where they are?
Teacher:	Jane?
Jane:	Because all the animals ran away.
Teacher:	Good, Jane! What makes you think that?
Jane:	Well, in the picture, all the other animals are gone.
Teacher:	That's right. Let's look at that page. The animals are gone, aren't they? What else do you notice about that picture? Billy?
Tom:	The crocodile looks happy.
Teacher:	She does look happy, doesn't she? Why do you think she looks happy?
Tom:	Well, she's grinning and her tongue is hanging out?
Teacher:	MMMMMmm, that's interesting. What is the crocodile doing there?
Molly:	Oh! Oh! The crocodile is licking its lips!
Teacher:	She is, isn't she? What happened?
Molly:	She ate the animals!
Teacher:	You know, I think the crocodile did eat the animals. So, why do you think the crocodile is asking, "Have you seen the parrot, the butterfly?" Jane?
Jane:	I think he's just being mean and joking.
Teacher:	Good thinking, Jane. I think so, too. What do you think, Molly? Yes? Tom?

Although this is a hypothetical discussion, I think it is typical of discussions that follow the Initiate-Respond-Evaluate pattern. The teacher has a definite objective in mind. She wants the children to understand that the animals are afraid of the crocodile and that the crocodile has eaten the other animals. Because the book does not make this explicit, it is an important aspect of the story to focus on in order to make sure that the children have comprehended. The teacher initiates the discussion with a question, the children respond, and the teacher evaluates the responses and then initiates with another question. She takes 15 of the 31 turns. In most cases the teacher's turns are longer than those of the children. This is the pattern of talk that dominates most traditional classrooms. Bellack et al. (1966) developed a description of this pattern that includes five rules (as summarized in Hoetker and Ahlbrand, 1969, p. 148):

1. Teachers are considerably more active [than students] in amount of verbal activity.

2. Teachers are responsible for structuring the lesson, soliciting responses. The students' primary task is to respond to the teacher's solicitations.

3. Bellack and Hoetker found that if talk was divided into four categories—structuring, solicitation, responding, and reacting—10 percent of the talk involved teachers structuring the lesson, whereas approximately 30 percent was teacher solicitation, about 27 percent involved student response, and about 25 percent involved teacher reaction.

4. The basic verbal interchange in the classroom is the solicitation-response.

5. By far the largest proportion of the discourse involved empirical [i.e.] factual meanings.

Hoetker and Ahlbrand concluded their review of the literature stating that this recitation pattern has shown remarkable stability since 1900. More recent research (Cazden, 1988; Marshall, Smagorinsky, & Smith, 1995; Mehan, 1979) indicates that the pattern has not yet disappeared. Notice that this format requires the same types of responses from all the children and that the content of the response as well as the correct answer is predetermined by the teacher. The range of participation in the discussion is very limited. If a child does not happen to be on the teacher's track, he or she is simply left behind. For example, early in the hypothetical discussion Sharon offers an answer that is not the one the teacher is searching for. The teacher's response is to move on to another child. One of the major shortcomings of traditional discussions is that they allow for only a very narrow range of participation. They do little to accommodate any type of diversity. The possible reasons for a child being on a separate track are plentiful: they include inability to read the text, as well as viewing the text from a cultural, ethnic, linguistic, or socioeconomic perspective that is different from the teachers'. Although this type of discussion may sometimes occur in a workshop classroom (for example, in a minilesson where the teacher has a specific agenda to communicate), much of the talk in workshop classrooms does not follow this pattern.

WORKSHOP DISCUSSION FORMATS

What follows is another discussion of *Have You Seen the Crocodile?* It actually occurred in the summer classroom during reading sharing. (An asterisk indicates a pause of one second.)

> Mary: This book is called *Have you Seen the Crocodile?* * It's like, uh, "*Pardon," Said the Giraffe,* [West] and, uh, this parrot keeps, this parrot keeps asking these critters, um, if they've seen the crocodile, and they

always answer, "No," and then um, and then he goes on to two and three. And it keeps going like this. So these three are asking [unintelligible] and now these four are asking [unintelligible]. And then * these five all asking that [unintelligible] frog [unintelligible]. And then * they're all so happy because none of them have seen the crocodile....Then, um, the crocodile sneaks up to the lion and says, "I've seen the crocodile," snaps the crocodile. And then it just, crocodile, then the crocodile says, "But have you, have anyone seen the, the parrot, the dragonfly, and the dragonfly and the bumblebee and the butterfly and the hummingbird and the frog...[unintelligible]."

Susan: Listen...

Mary: Looks like he licked...

Karen: He only...

Mary: He licked his lips. It looks like he ate 'em.

Karen: He only ate, he only ate, he only ate the parrot.

Child: [unintelligible]

Mary: He might eat 'em all.
He might of eat 'em all.

Child: Yeah and then he asked.

Wes: Hey. What's that?

Mary: Yeah. He's asking everyone else. Comments or questions?

Child: [unintelligible]

Child: I think, uh, I like it. [long pause]

Roller: Remember, part of the importance is that everybody comment. Mary?

Child: [unintelligible]

Roller: I think that picture with the tongue hanging out of his mouth is one of the really great pictures.

Karen: Me too.

Susan: Me too.

Mary: I like the parrot and the hummingbird.

Susan: I like [unintelligible].

Jimmy: I like the part when the alligators—I thought he was gonna bite the one bird 'cause he looked like...

Peter: Uh, the parrot?

Jimmy: Yeah. Yeah right.

Child: No.

Peter: Yup.

Jimmy: Right there.

Peter: It's a parrot.

Jimmy: Is he gonna bite him or what?

Child: No.

Mary: I think he ate 'em all.

Bobby: No.

Karen: Uuh, Uuh, just the parrot.

Bobby: They, they just hide.

Roller: Well, it's kind of hard to tell, but that alligator sure looks like it's lickin' its lips.

Karen: Just the parrot and he ate the [unintelligible].

Mary: Yeah, and he asked where all of them are, all of them.

Karen: No, uuh, uuh, he asked all of them where the parrot was.

Wes: He's asking where they are.

Child: [unintelligible] that's fuss.

Wes: [unintelligible] he's asking where they are so he can find 'em.

Jimmy: And eat 'em.

Roller: Read that page. I think he asked after every one of them, didn't he?

Mary: But he only sees, "Has anyone seen the parrot and the dragonfly and the, and the bumblebee and the butterfly and the hummingbird and the frog?" I don't know. He's lickin' his lips like he's going to eat them.

Holly: I know, but didn't you see the—I know, but didn't you see the...

Mary: [unintelligible] and so his lips get ready to go after 'em.

Holly: I know, but didn't you see the...

Mary: Or he ate one of 'em.

Holly: I know, but...

Roller: This is the kind of thing that you can never really know. I think each person decides what they think happens.

Mary: You could write part two of this book.

Child: What?

Mary: You could write part two of this book.

Roller: You could write part two of that book, couldn't you? It'd be a good thing to do. OK, do you want to choose somebody to share?

Although the content of the two discussions is quite similar, the structure of the discussions is different. The teachers' roles differ dramatically. I spoke only 6 of the 53 turns. During two of those turns I did some structuring. In one turn I reminded, "Remember, part of the importance is that everybody comment," and later I asked, "OK, do you want to choose someone to share?" signaling that the child's sharing turn was over. At one turn, I directed a student to read part of the text to clarify a point. Two other turns were comments that contributed to the ongoing discussion and focused attention on the illustration. Notice that in the end, I did not take a stand relative to whether the crocodile ate all the animals or just the parrot. This was a situation where there was no sure answer. In fact, when I read the book, I assumed that the crocodile had eaten all the animals, but the children's discussion helped me recognize other interpretations. The discussion format did not predetermine the children's responses.

COMPARING DISCUSSION FORMATS

Traditional classroom discussions and workshop format discussions differ markedly. In the second discussion I described from the SRP classroom, the children are talking more, and for the most part they are in charge of the directions the conversation takes. The discussions are different because although teachers in each class may have a similar goal—to improve children's comprehension—they conceptualize reaching that goal in different ways. In a traditional classroom, the teacher usually approaches comprehension teaching by making sure that the children understand the story in the way that he or she has understood the story. Marshall, Smagorinsky, and Smith (1995) conducted observational studies that examined classroom discussions that followed the typical Initiate-Respond-Evaluate pattern. They concluded that the teacher in traditional discussions was establishing the meaning or interpretation of the text. What students learned in these discussions were particular interpretations of particular texts.

In IRE discussions, it is the teacher who does the complex work of meaning construction and interpretation, while students follow along, fill in blanks, and arrive at the teacher's predetermined end point. In my first discussion example, the teacher was carefully guiding children toward canonical interpretations, calling attention to relevant facts, and leading them to appropriate inferences. In the book sharing discussion from the SRP classroom, I served as a facilitator. I structured the session and directed the children to return to the text for verification, but I did not have a particular end point in mind. The children did the thinking. They questioned what happened to the animals and offered plausible interpretations that I had not even thought of. Although some of the same things happened in the two discussions—in both, the teacher had the children return to the text for verification and the children drew inferences—in the reading sharing discussion, the children ultimately constructed the meaning for themselves. I did not construct meaning for them, and they did not try to guess what I wanted them to say.

In reading sharing discussions in a workshop environment a child takes the first turn. It is what the *child* chooses to say about the book that determines the content of the discussion. Because the first turn is structured—a child gives the title and author, says something about the book or reads from it, and asks for comments or questions—every child can learn the format and participate. But the loose generic structure that follows allows for much more variability in participation than in traditional formats. One discussion we had in SRP following the sharing of a book was only five turns. Short discussions like this one often include quick exchanges in which children ask and answer questions such as "Why did you pick that book?" and "What was your favorite page?" Another discussion lasted 164 turns and covered several substantive topics. Sometimes talkative children like Mary give long and detailed explanations of stories, whereas other children take short initial turns. In one discussion, for example, Randy simply said, "This is called *Around and Around*. My favorite part is 'Stop! Stop! I'm going to get sick!'" (The book *Round and Round* by Joy Cowley is about a character running around and around various objects, and at the end the character gets dizzy.) Then after Randy's opening, I suggested that he read the whole book to the children because it was short. I knew he could do it because I had worked with him and watched him practice. Reading the book well to his classmates was a positive experience for him. The sharing format accommodates variability in ways that traditional formats do not.

If our intention is to have students learn particular interpretations of texts, then the IRE pattern is efficient, and we should use it. However, I think our purposes in classroom discussion go far beyond single interpretations of particular texts. What I really want to do in classroom discussions is help children create meaning from text. I want them to learn to create their own interpretations, and I want to meet each child at a place appropriate for him or her. I want sharing discussions to be a major tool in creating a classroom environment that embraces differences.

BELIEFS ABOUT DISCUSSION

Giving children the space to make their own meanings and the chance to do the tasks that will move them forward requires that we listen to children's talk and respond to each child as an individual. However, it is difficult to leave traditional teacher-directed patterns behind. On many occasions, when I decided that I was not going to do the talking, I found that my students had nothing to say. I have led, participated in, and observed many such discussions, and they are painful. As an observer, I could feel the teacher wanting the children to talk and could see the children's bewilderment. As a teacher, I was often daunted by students' silence and more often than not responded by talking more than I intended. We are conditioned to the IRE pattern; we need some specific help with ways to break the pattern. In the next section, I will talk about some specific strategies I have learned to encourage talk. Much of what I have learned is the result of conversations and work with Penny Beed. Penny is a professor at University of Northern Iowa and a former doctoral student advisee of mine. She has studied sharing discussions in her own classroom and has worked with me at SRP in many capacities. Before Penny and I learned about strategies to encourage talk, we had to change three beliefs.

First, we had to change the belief that experiencing silence during class is wasting time. Silence during good discussions rarely indicates wasted time; in fact, silence is often productive. Remember, many students do not come to discussions with well-formed interpretations of the text. Silence allows students valuable thinking time. Although a silence of up to three seconds seems excruciatingly long to us, it is really a very short amount of time to allow students to do the work of meaning construction. There are at least two places where silence is useful: after a question and after a response. Silence after a response signals that it is acceptable for another student to respond to the first student, rather than automatically returning to the questioner or discussion leader.

The second belief we changed is about our notions of discussion content. We learned to have reasonable expectations for children's discussions. Children's perspectives and life experiences are quite different than ours, and frequently the issues that interest them are not the ones that we would choose to raise for discussion. When we first made the commitment to promoting more student talk, what we seemed to want was the same talk *we* would have elicited without us doing the work. However, when we analyzed the discussions that occurred in our workshop classrooms, we found that the discussions varied widely. Sometimes they were lively and the content substantive, as in the crocodile discussion. However, sometimes the lively discussions seemed almost content free, sometimes discussions that had substantive content were less than lively, and sometimes the discussions were both content free and lifeless. (See also the 1994 article I coauthored with Penny Beed.)

It required a good deal of reflection and study to come to terms with the fact that our classroom discussions did not always live up to our ideal. We eventually understood that if we demanded discussions that met our expectations, we would seriously circumscribe important options available to the children. While sometimes children's discussions do not fit an ideal prototype, they usually accomplish important objectives for the children. Lively "content-free" (from our perspective) discussions actually are not always content free from the children's perspectives. The talk is lively because the content is important to them. Substantive but lifeless discussions often lead to the establishment of important information, and lifeless and content-free discussions often allow less confident and less verbal children to participate in the sharing. We decided that the more flexible format of reading sharing was crucial to meeting the instructional and personal needs of a variety of children.

The third belief we abandoned is the notion that student talk wastes time. Often, we acted as though it took children too long to say what they wanted to say; sometimes we even finished their sentences. We learned to believe that listening to students provides valuable information. We need to listen carefully to determine the meaning the children are trying to reach. We cannot help children develop their meanings if we do not hear those meanings. It is very easy in workshop settings for teachers to focus on specific agendas for children or to have specific goals. When teachers get preoccupied with their own agendas, often problems can occur. The following example happened after Randy's sharing of *Round and Round*.

Randy was one of the poorest readers and shyest children in my SRP class. His sharing of *Round and Round* was his first attempt at talking about a book with the class. I was delighted when he volunteered, and I encouraged him during the initial part of his turn. I had an agenda in mind, however. I wanted the children to use patterns in their writing. So, after a few comments there was a silence and I said,

> Um, I guess I should have said this during comments. You know, these are the kind of books that are easy for kids to read, but sometimes they aren't as interesting to some of you, but you could make it more interesting if, instead of putting around and around this [the object in the book], and around and—you could choose your own things and write a new book for the class, and that would be a really nice kind of book to have on the yellow bookcase back there. The one that's for your books.

This response to a struggling, reluctant, shy sharer essentially said: "Well, that was pretty boring, but we might be able to make it more interesting." How could I be so insensitive? The answer is that I was not focused on Randy, and I was not listening to him. Instead, I was looking at his sharing as an instance of the sharing of a patterned book. I had been waiting for someone to share a patterned book because I wanted to show the children that they could use patterns in their writing. And so I responded in a way that was entirely inappropriate. It was fortunate that there was another adult in the classroom at the time who helped the situation by immediately pointing out that this was exactly what Randy was doing.

I share this example to emphasize the need to listen to each child and focus on what is happening in the ongoing talk. Any teaching that is done during talk must come out of the talk itself. Teachers must listen if they are to teach effectively. Although teachers may have agendas and ideas about skills that might be taught effectively, letting teacher agendas dictate the direction of children's talk can be disastrous.

CONVERSATIONAL STRATEGIES TO ENCOURAGE STUDENT TALK

Listening to children is one of the hardest lessons we have learned in SRP. It is hard not to talk all the time. At first we did not know what to do if we did not ask question after question. What follows is a series of specific alternatives—conversational strategies—we have learned to help open discussions in ways that encourage student talk and keep the talk going.

Letting Students Open Discussions

There are several strategies that will work for opening discussions. A simple one is to let a student take the first turn. This is easily accomplished in reading sharing sessions, where it is the student's responsibility to share some sort of response about his or her book. However, even when students are not in charge, it is easy enough to put them in this role by beginning discussions by asking students what they thought. Questions such as "What did you think of...?" "Did you like ...?" and "What was your favorite part?" are all effective ways to turn the initial response to the children.

Using a Declarative Statement

Another possibility for encouraging student talk is offered by Dillon (1984, as cited in Alvermann, Dillon, & O'Brien, 1987). He reported a discussion about the events leading to the Nazi takeover of Germany. The discussion leader opened by saying, "From the start, the Weimar Republic was faced with insurmountable problems." He simply made a declarative statement and then waited for students to elaborate. Another option is for the teacher to offer his or her own opinion and let students respond to that. Statements and questions that open discussions should be as open ended as possible. This statement about the takeover of Germany introduced a topic but did not confine the students' responses, as would happen if the discussion leader had begun with a question such as, "Can you name five of the problems that the Weimar Republic faced?" or perhaps, "What were some of the problems that the Weimar Republic faced?"

Really Listening to Children

Probably the most important thing for teachers to do in encouraging talk is to have an honest interest in what students are saying or trying to say. Children's talk is fascinating if we learn to listen *to* them rather than *for* something. We must be genuinely committed to leading from behind. This often means abandoning our preconceived notion of what is appropriate and instead watching for what is actually happening. Listening is the major tool we have for attending to individual differences, which is particularly important when we are dealing with children who differ from ourselves—in ability or in cultural, ethnic, racial, linguistic, or socioeconomic background. At SRP, we have found that transcribing conversations periodically is one way to sharpen our listening skills; seeing conversations on paper captures them in a way that makes it easier to learn from them.

Taking the Short Turn

When we think of sustaining student talk, we think of it as learning how to take the "short turn." As we noted earlier, traditional classroom discussions are characterized by an imbalance in teacher-student talk: teachers take the long turns and students take the short ones. Marshall, Smagorinsky, & Smith (1995) found that teachers' turns were two to five times longer than student turns and that, on the average, the conversation lead was returned to the teacher after each of the student's contributions.

So how can teachers learn to take the short turn and encourage students to deliver their messages in as full and complete a way as possible? Tough (1985) refers to these "short turns" as sustaining strategies, as follows:

1. Practice wait time—don't jump in when a student finishes speaking. Remaining silent and maintaining eye contact suggests that you are waiting for more.

2. Use nonverbal gestures such as head nodding, smiling, chuckling, and so forth that suggest you are both attending to and enjoying the student's contribution.

3. Make short comments such as "Really?" "Oh?" or "What else?" that encourage the child to continue.

4. Simply say "MMmmmmmmm" or "uh huh?"

5. Repeat the child's last few words with a rising intonation that suggests you would like him or her to continue talking.

Each one of these strategies will constitute a turn and put the burden of speaking on the students in the conversation.

In School Classrooms

The suggestions in this chapter for opening and sustaining discussion are intended for any classroom. Penny Beed and I have used them to change the discussion patterns in our university classes as well as in the morning SRP classroom. Sharing discussions are an important part of any classroom that successfully accommodates differences. At SRP we have a short time to work with the children, and sharing discussions about books are our predominant focus.

However, these discussions sometimes lack depth because no one other than the child who is sharing has read the book being discussed (see Roller & Beed, 1994). We balance the discussion that occurs during sharing with the talk that occurs during oral literature. When we read to the children we can talk about a common text as a class, which can add the depth that is sometimes missing when the responders have not read the text. In school classrooms where 30 rather than 5½ consecutive weeks are available to work with the same children, we would probably give the discussion of common texts even more attention. We would be sure that ample discussion accompanied oral literature, and we would encourage situations where children met together to discuss a book they had all read.

This does not necessarily require assigning children to read specific books nor having everyone in the class choose to read one of several available choices. In a workshop classroom, children inevitably talk about the books they read, and other children become interested and read them as well. One of my practicum students used a system of entering the books the children read in a computer database that sorted by book. She easily found all the children who had read a book and convened them for a discussion, thus balancing individual choice with the benefits of commonality.

In all classrooms, teachers must first and foremost be listeners. The teacher's agendas and interventions must arise from what the children are actually doing and saying. Teachers must not become so involved in their teaching that they lose sight of what a child is trying to do. The most important word in a teacher's vocabulary is *listen*. Listening allows us to respond to children in ways that accommodate their variability.

Chapter Six

Direct Instruction
Occurs in Context

with Penny L. Beed and Sylvia Forsyth

THE SINGLE most damaging misconception of whole language or work-shop format instruction is that direct instruction should play no part in the classroom. Much of the misunderstanding surrounding direct instruction results from an inappropriate equating of skills instruction with the direct instruction methods frequently used to deliver it. Skills instruction involves segmenting knowledge into its component parts and teaching each in isolation, as discussed earlier. Skills have been defined as anything from pronouncing the short "a" sound to getting the main idea or drawing conclusions. In traditional classrooms skills are directly instructed using teacher-led lessons followed by myriad worksheets for guided and independent practice.

Whole language proponents object to this type of skills instruction and to the specific direct instruction model used to deliver it. They make statements such as "Whole language does not mean teaching skills in context" (Edelsky, Altwerger, & Flores, 1991, p. 340). These statements are directed at skills teaching and the specific direct instruction model just described. It is unfortunate that the statements are often misinterpreted. "Not teaching skills in context" is confused with "not teaching skills at all" or "not using direct teaching methods associated with skills teaching." The resulting interpretation is that "whole language does not mean teaching," and many whole language neophytes find themselves afraid to teach.

Teaching skills does not necessarily mean segmenting language into parts and teaching each in isolation, and direct instruction does not necessarily mean lengthy teacher-led lessons and children inundated in worksheets. Rather, skills such as skipping an unknown word while reading, using sound-letter relationships to help pronunciation, and rereading to make sense of text can be taught holistically as children engage in real reading. We can use alternative ways of implementing direct instruction that substitute brief lessons and teacher interaction for lengthy lessons and worksheets. Isolated segmented skills exercises *are not* effective or appropriate; there is too much evidence that skills taught in isolation do not transfer to other situations. However, intentional teaching of reading skills is an *essential* part of all classrooms and particularly critical for struggling readers.

It seems almost silly that I should have to say that intentional teaching is essential. But I must say it because so much of what has been said and written about the changing role of the teacher in whole language classrooms has been interpreted to mean that teachers should not teach. The teacher is a guide, a coach, a facilitator. He or she creates environments in which children discover and learn. I wholeheartedly support this view of the teacher. However, I object to these descriptions if they are interpreted to mean that teachers should not teach.

The idea that teachers should not teach is a mistaken extension of the early language-acquisition research that shows that children learn language incidentally in conversation with the individuals who surround them. The thinking seems to be that if children can learn language incidentally, they can learn anything incidentally. There are two problems with this thinking. First, there is direct instruction in language learning. Few children, for example, learn language conventions such as saying "hello and goodbye" and "please and thank you" without direct instruction. A parent directs a child: "Say 'bye bye,' Johnny. We're going now" or "Tell the woman, 'thank you.'" Second, parents teach children many things as well as language. Sometimes a child learns incidentally, but sometimes a child does not. There are few children who learn to tie their shoes without someone directly and intentionally teaching them how. Parents usually choose a sensible approach to learning: they are pleased when their child learns incidentally, but when the child does not learn incidentally, they help him or her by directly teaching.

One of the ubiquitous findings in reading and learning research is that some children learn better with direct instruction. The mistaken belief that there is no direct instruction in whole language classrooms is largely responsible for many struggling readers being provided alternative "non–whole language" instructional environments. Many professionals say that whole language is all right for children who do not have learning problems, but it will not work for children who are struggling because they need direct instruction. I would argue that everyone needs direct instruction in some things, some of the time, and that a whole language classroom is an ideal setting for providing appropriate direct instruction for all children, including struggling readers.

To me direct instruction means intentional teaching. Many models for direct instruction exist, but I use one (loosely derived from Hunter, 1976) that includes six components, which do not necessarily occur in sequential order. The components include (1) introduction, (2) modeling and explanation, (3) feedback, (4) guided practice, (5) independent practice, and (6) evaluation. A central component of direct instruction is the "gradual release of responsibility"— the teacher first holds the responsibility for performing the strategy and gradually lets the child assume the responsibility until the child performs the strategy independently (Pearson & Gallagher, 1983). Historically, the gradual release of responsibility has been achieved by having children do worksheets, first with guidance and then independently. Evaluation consisted of marking worksheets and checking students on end-of-level tests. In the SRP classroom, I use a combination of minilessons and strategic scaffolding to implement the six direct instruction components. Strategic scaffolding (which I will explain in more detail later) refers to the conversational moves teachers make when they are interacting with children one-on-one (Beed, Hawkins, & Roller, 1991). This conception of direct instruction is different from other common conceptions in which the guided and independent practice and evaluation involve the use of worksheets. However, the instruction I use is direct and I do intentionally teach.

I use direct instruction primarily for teaching reading strategies such as what to do when you are confused, how to figure out what an unknown word means, and what to do if you come to a word you cannot pronounce. Because of the historic connotations of the term "skills," which are connected with traditional teaching methods, I use the term "strategies." I also prefer the term strategies because it has the strong suggestion of an action taken in context and used flexibly. I usually do the introduction and modeling and explanation components of direct instruction in short minilessons. The *introduction* is an orienting step that makes the purpose of the upcoming instruction clear to the learner. In this component I name the strategy and explain its purpose. During *modeling and explanation*, I provide several examples of the strategy and explain my use of it by verbalizing my thinking as I go. *Feedback* involves constantly checking to see if the children are following and understanding the instruction; it occurs in every component.

The remaining components—*guided practice, independent practice,* and *evaluation*—usually occur during individual conferences as children are engaged in their reading. These components are crucial to the gradual release of responsibility that must occur if a child is to become an independent reader. Strategic scaffolding is my major tool for transferring responsibility. It is a way to achieve the gradual release of responsibility through one-on-one interaction rather than through worksheets. It involves six levels of actions made by the teacher, which I will explain in detail in the section on strategic scaffolding.

MINILESSONS

A minilesson is a very short lesson (usually 2 to 5 minutes and always less than 10). I learned the term from Calkins's book *The Art of Teaching Writing* (1986) in the chapter titled "Don't Be Afraid to Teach." At SRP minilessons occur in several settings. At the beginning of workshop time I often take five minutes to teach a lesson to the whole group. Other times minilessons occur as short impromptu segments of conferences. The tutoring sessions described more fully in the final section of this chapter also include minilessons. My large-group minilessons do not include guided and independent practice; practice takes too long and is usually not appropriate for many of the children. Basically the minilesson includes only the instruction and modeling and explanation components of direct instruction.

The following minilesson occurred with Sung, a second-language speaker of English, and her tutor, Miss Kearney. Sung had mastered the sound-letter correspondences of English but often did not know the meanings of words. One of our goals was for her to learn how to figure out the meaning of words from the context. Sung, her tutor, and I were all working on this.

One day Sung was reading Mem Fox's book *Guess What?* Each page has a sentence that asks a question. On the following page the question is answered and another question is posed. When Sung was reading the text "Has she got a cat that is really sleek and black? Guess!" she had difficulty with the word "sleek." Although she pronounced it, it was clear from her intonation that she did not know what the word meant. Her tutor introduced a strategy—"think aloud"—by saying, "Let's see how we can figure out what sleek means. Could we think about cats?" Sung agreed and the tutor continued modeling and explaining:

> Well, there is something we can do to figure out what a word means even if we can say the word, but we don't know what it means. It's called "think aloud." You must think aloud whatever is in your head and talk about it. Try to think about

things you already know about the word's meaning. Like I said we could think about cats. I think, black cats, and maybe witches. I'd look at the picture and, hmm, it's pretty obvious he's black, and they already said that, so sleek probably doesn't mean black. I don't think they'd say it twice. Hm. What does sleek mean? I'd look at him. He's got big eyes.

At this point Sung offered, "Scary?" Her tutor replied, "Well, I'd look at him again and think, does he look scary?" Sung then said, "No. Cute?" Miss Kearney continued modeling the strategy:

Yeah, he's kind of cute. I might go back and read and put "cute" in "sleek's" place. Does she have a cat that's really cute and black? Hmmm. It doesn't seem to make sense, a witch having a cute cat. Maybe I could look at his body?"

"Skinny?" then questioned Sung. Her tutor said, "Yeah, he is skinny. And shiny."

They continued the discussion, and Miss Kearney ended by summarizing, "That's one way to go about finding out what a word we don't know means." When she asked Sung for feedback, Sung summarized, "Um, you kinda described, you kind of like, say like, does it have shiny fur? Is it like this? That?" Sung was also able to label the strategy and tell when to use it: "When we, um, say a word but, and we don't know what kinda, what it is, what it means."

This was an excellent minilesson. Notice that Miss Kearney did not take the strategy and break it down in steps and that the lesson occurred as Sung was reading a book that she very much wanted to read. The purpose of the lesson was clear: Sung needed to know the meaning of "sleek," an important word in the story she was reading. The strategy was labeled "think aloud," and Miss Kearney did an excellent job of modeling the strategy. She returned to Sung for feedback to make sure that Sung was understanding the instruction. On subsequent occasions, which I will talk about later, they practiced the strategy until Sung was able to use it independently. Figure 3 on page 74 presents two more examples of minilessons.

STRATEGIC SCAFFOLDING

Scaffolding is a procedure for gradually reducing the level of teacher participation (which in the initial stages may be very high, as it was in the previous example) and gradually increasing the student's responsibility. Bruner (1975) noted it as a natural feature of parents' interactions with their children. In situations when a child encounters difficulties, the parent offers help. The kind of help offered depends on the parent's estimate of what the child is capable of in this particular sit-

Figure 3   Minilessons

Minilesson #1

Introduction: "Yesterday in class I noticed that when David was reading a book about sharks, he was writing some of the words. I asked him why he was writing the words and he said that it helped him remember them. Writing down words does help some people, and we can use a word bank as a way to organize this writing."

Modeling with explanation: "There are several ways you can organize your writing and save the words. You can use a notebook, index box, bookmark, or word ring."

Show an example of each and explain how it was constructed.

Feedback: Ask children to summarize why they might want to write down words and how they would go about saving them.

Minilesson #2

Introduction: "Peter, I noticed that yesterday this word was in your story, 'will.' For most of the story you called that word 'do.' That was fine because the story was making sense. But when you came to the last page you called that word 'will.' It was in the sentence....What happened? How did you know it was 'will' and not 'do?'"

Modeling with explanation: "Hm. How can you tell this word is 'will' and not 'do?' I'll look at this word and copy it. It starts with a 'w.' 'W' makes a /w/ sound:/w/ /w/ /w/ill. 'Do' starts with /d/, not /w/. So 'will' has to be the right one. I can figure out which word by looking at the beginning sound."

Feedback: "Is that the way you could tell? By looking at the beginning sound?"

---

uation. Strategic scaffolding can be used to teach any kind of strategy. For example, a sales clerk can use scaffolding to train a new employee. Hawkins (Beed, Hawkins, & Roller, 1991, p. 632) used scaffolding to teach a child a book introduction technique designed to improve comprehension. She taught John to use six prereading questions, as follows, to focus his reading on meaning.

1. What do you know from the title of the story?

2. What do you want to know after reading the title?

3. What do you already know about the ideas in the title?

4. What do you know from the illustration?

5. What do you want to know after seeing the illustration?

6. What do you already know about the ideas in the illustration?

Scaffolding is a ubiquitous occurrence in the informal teaching that occurs in all the settings of our lives.

Penny Beed, Sylvia Forsyth, who is currently completing her doctoral dissertation with me at the University of Iowa, and I have adapted Wood's scaffolding levels (Wood, Bruner, & Ross, 1976; Wood, Wood, & Middleton, 1978) to six levels that are useful in describing one-on-one reading interactions. The following levels describe actions to be taken by the teacher:

1. assuming total responsibility by solving the problem

2. inviting the child's participation

3. cueing a specific strategy

4. cueing general strategy use

5. reinforcing the child's independent use of the strategy

6. building metacognitive awareness

The important thing to note about the levels is that in the earlier stages teacher participation is high and student participation is low. Gradually the balance reverses until student participation is high and teacher participation is low.

I will provide several examples of each of these levels, but I want to begin with an example that includes several levels. Notice that early in the following example, I responded to Andy's requests for help at scaffolding levels one and two but that as the interaction continued my responses moved to levels three and four. Also notice that when Andy was unable to respond to my initial scaffold, I quickly moved to an easier level. Over time, as the child becomes more independent, the interactions may move from level one to level six, but depending on the situation, problem, and context, the interactions may begin at various levels.

I was reading Bill Martin's *Brown Bear, Brown Bear, What Do You See?* with Andy. He had never read the book before, and when he chose it, he pointed to the title. "I don't know these words," he said. I responded, "Oh, that's *Brown Bear, Brown Bear, What Do You See?* It's a great book" (teacher responsibility).

Andy read the opening page fluently but hesitated when he got to the word "Redbird" on the second page: "I see a Redbird looking at me." He sounded the "r" and guessed "rabbit."

"That's good. Keep going!" I encouraged (inviting participation). I helped him with the words "looking at me" (teacher responsibility). When he turned the page, I asked, "What was it?" (inviting participation).

"Bird," replied Andy.

"What color bird?" (inviting participation).

"Red."

As I pointed to the word "Redbird," I said, "It's a Redbird, isn't it?" (teacher responsibility).

He then read "Redbird, Redbird, What do you see?" fluently but hesitated when he came to "yellow duck" on the next page. I *cued a specific strategy* by telling him he could skip it. He did and then read fluently until he came to the next animal. He stopped and told me he didn't know the words. At this point I modeled skipping the words by saying "blank blank" for "blue horse" as I read the sentence, and then I explained by showing him that the next page would provide help with a picture (teacher responsibility).

The third time he stopped at the animal name I said, "You can..." (general cue), and Andy skipped the words and continued reading. The next time he stopped and said he didn't know the word, I used a *general cue*, "What could you do to help you figure out that word?"

He looked up startled and said, "Huh, what?" I don't think anyone had ever asked him a question like that. I repeated myself, and he said, "Sound it out."

"Sound it out is one thing. You could skip it and say the next word," I responded (cueing the specific strategy).

On the next page he stopped again and said he didn't know a word. I asked, "What can you do?" (general cue).

He responded, "Sound it out."

I invited him to add the direction "skip it" by saying, "And if you can't sound it out, you can..." (general cue).

Andy continued, "Skip it."

On the next page he stopped again, and I asked what he could do (general cue). He answered, "Sound it out or just skip it."

The next time he paused, I simply said, "Hmmmm" (general cue).

Andy whispered to himself, "I could just skip it or, uh, sound it out." He skipped it and continued reading.

In the span of one short book, the responsibility for reading on to aid word identification ("skip it") shifted from me to Andy. This shift in responsibility and the way that it occurred is critical for effective scaffolding. It is unlikely that Andy fully acquired the skip-it strategy in one lesson. Over time, I might need to review the strategy, cue it, and use the remaining two steps—affirming his strategy use and having him build his metacognitive awareness—by having him talk about his spontaneous strategy use. Always the objective is to give Andy just the amount of help he needs to be successful and gradually arrive at the point where he no longer needs any help. I included this example because it demonstrates a number of scaffolding levels accomplished in a relatively short period of time. However, scaffolding does not always move at this pace, and it does not always include every level.

Before I move into a fuller discussion of strategic scaffolding levels, I offer a caution: the most important thing to know about direct instruction is when to offer it. Too much instruction can destroy the story. I particularly remember one child who was reading a book that was too difficult. He was having problems with many words, and the tutor was taking advantage of each one as an opportunity to scaffold word-recognition techniques. She did not seem to notice that every time she prompted, the child slapped the table, sighed, or protested. The child no longer wanted to read the book, but the teacher agenda of scaffolding word recognition drove the session. The child was right. The book was too difficult for him to gain meaning. Meaning is always the point. If the teaching takes the focus away from meaning making for too long, there is too much teaching and not enough meaning making. The sensible thing to have done in this situation was for the tutor to finish reading the book or to find another book. The child's slaps, sighs, and protests (as well as the high proportion of unknown words) were telling the teacher that she and the child were headed in different directions. Scaffolding the child in directions that the child is resisting is not productive and, in fact, can be damaging to the child's motivation to read.

Teacher Responsibility

Sometimes the first level of scaffolding means providing children with difficult words when they are reading. Typically I supply children with proper names if they are having difficulty. I also offer words that I estimate are outside the child's conceptual vocabulary. For example, when I read a book with James, he hesitated on the word "custard." I suspected he was not familiar with custard and said, "I don't think you probably know that. That's another word for pudding.

It's called 'custard.'" For another child I supplied the word "distress" saying, "OK. I don't think you know this word. It's 'distress.' When you're distressed you're all upset." I also give children words when for one reason or another they are reading too difficult text. One child tried to read Bill Martin's *Polar Bear, Polar Bear, What Do You See?* after having success with *Brown Bear, Brown Bear*. However, *Polar Bear* has many difficult words. I supplied words such as "flamingo," "braying," and "boa constrictor." Giving children a word is the highest level of teacher responsibility.

Another way of taking full responsibility is to both model and explain strategy use. I did that in the example with Andy reading *Brown Bear, Brown Bear*. First, I read the sentence saying "blank, blank" for "blue horse." Then I turned the page and explained that he could skip the words because on the next page he would find a picture that would help with the words.

Inviting Participation

Inviting participation is almost automatic when working one-on-one with a child. We seem to stop naturally and let the child make some contribution. We read along, taking most of the responsibility, and pause when we are sure that the child will be able to read the next little bit. Often the invitation is offered by reading and pausing as it was several times in a conference with Manny. We were reading *Danger!* by Joy Cowley. The text has a repetitive pattern: "Look out for _____. They are full of _____." The ending words of the two sentences rhyme as well (for example, "chairs/bears" and "boxes/foxes"). Three times during the reading, I read the sentence leaving out the final word of the sentence and waited for Manny to fill in and continue. At one point I said, "This one's hard. 'Look out for ditches.'" I paused and when he didn't begin I said, "Go ahead." Later in the conference, I reversed roles and said, "Mmm. And this one's hard, too. You start."

Another common example of inviting participation is giving the child an initial consonant sound. Manny was reading the text from *Bike Lesson* by Stan and Janice Berenstain, which read, "Yes, that is what you should not do!" He read, "Yes, that is what you're not /ssssup/ supposed not /s/...I don't know that one." I started to say, "OK, what's the—" because I think I was going to cue Manny to look at the beginning sound. But midsentence, I decided he might not know the /sh/ sound. I asked, "Do you know the first two letters?" When I got no response I said, "s-h together makes the sound /sh/. /Sh/...." Manny continued on "shhhould" and figured out "should."

78

Cueing a Specific Strategy

Inviting participation can gradually shift so that more responsibility rests with the child. Cueing a specific strategy basically tells the child what to do and then has the child do it. The following example of cueing a specific strategy occurred when Miss Kearney was working with Sung on the word "hearth." They had used several strategies and Miss Kearney asked Sung to think about what they had done the day before, but Sung did not initiate thinking aloud. Miss Kearney said, "Hmm, 'hearth.' What does hearth mean? Can you think aloud here?" Sung responded to the cue by using the strategy. She said,

> Heat. This hearth, uh, she I might think it's kinda the same, and this little girl is kinda getting these things, burning straws. So she must be by the fire and this thing must keep the family warm during the winter. So, it must be kinda like a little place to keep the fire in.

Cueing General Strategy Use

At the next level, rather than prompt a specific strategy, I provide a general prompt hoping that the child can come up with a strategy on his or her own. The shift here makes the child not only perform the strategy but also identify which strategy is appropriate. For example, Donald was reading the text "No sense waiting around for the rain" from Carolyn B. Otto's *That Sky, That Rain*, and he substituted "seasons" for "sense." When he paused, I said, "OK. Did that make sense to you?"(general cue). Then he went back and reread the sentence correctly.

The general prompt "Did that make sense?" is one I use frequently because it communicates to the child the importance of making reading make sense and suggests that he or she must take some action to make it do so. Because the particular action was not specified, more responsibility rested with Donald, and the general cue moved him closer to independence.

On another occasion shortly after Manny figured out "should" in the example earlier, he came to the word "showed" in the sentence "You showed me how." He substituted "should" for "showed" several times and there was a lengthy pause. I asked, "What can you do when you get stuck?" (general cue). I was briefly distracted by another child and when I returned my attention to Manny, he read the sentence fluently. Manny also was able to take specific action when given the general prompt.

Reinforcing the Child's Strategy Use

The next scaffolding level is reinforcing the child's independent use of the strategy. At this level the child has full responsibility for identifying and using the strategy without a prompt. The teacher merely comments on what the child has done. This is a level of support I use frequently. For example, Conrad was reading *The Paper Crane* by Molly Bang, and there were several, not very critical, words that he had trouble with. I responded, "I liked what you did here. You read this part fine. You got a little stuck on here. And then you just skipped and went on. Now do you have the sense of what's going on on this page?" Conrad answered yes and gave a brief synopsis. I continued,

> So really this word isn't too important because you understand what's happening in the story. Actually that word is unusual. But I think that's a good idea. When you know you're understanding a story, sometimes it's OK to skip a word.

In another instance when Ned self-corrected I said, "That's really good. You only had one place where you said...here at 'known,' you said something other than 'known' and then you went back and corrected it all by yourself."

One time I was asking James to use his finger to track print because he had not yet made a word to print match. As he was reading a well-practiced text, he did use his finger and made a number of self-corrections. I shared my running record with him and said,

> James, I am so pleased. You know what you're doing that really is tremendous? See all these SCs [self-corrections marked on the running record] I'm getting because you're using that finger? You're going back and making things right that weren't right the first time through. That's really good. Keep going.

Building Metacognitive Awareness of Strategies

A final move that forces children's independence is to have *them* identify and explain their own strategies. At this level the child is responsible for knowing and using the appropriate strategies and also knowing what they know. I sometimes ask children to explain to me how they read a particular word correctly. For instance, after Manny correctly read "showed" in the earlier example, I asked, "How'd you get that?" He pointed to "should" in the previous sentence where I had helped him with the /sh/ sound and said, "I went back and looked at that one." I commented, "The s-h. And it reminded you of the /sh/ sound? That's a great strategy."

On another occasion, Anita struggled with the word "ducked" but got it. I asked, "How did you know? How did you get 'ducked'? Can you explain it to me?" Anita answered, "'Ducked,' I went, first I sounded out, then I know it didn't make sense, then I just got 'duck.' It made sense."

Sometimes I ask the children to find some places where they had problems and explain how they solved them. Tommie explained that he was able to figure out "pretend," which he had originally called "protect," by saying, "Because we pretend we're dancing." I elaborated, "It made sense. So you used the sense, and it made the word make sense."

When I asked Robbie to find a place in his book where he used good strategies, he pointed to the word "market" and said "market." I asked him to tell me what happened with that word. He said that he thought about what was happening and then sounded out.

Sung was working hard on using prior knowledge and context to figure out the meaning of words. When I asked her what she did when she did not understand a word, she referred to a specific incident when Miss Kearney had helped her figure out the meaning of the word "steady." She indicated that she reread it a few times, and then she and Miss Kearney talked about the story and she decided that "steady" meant "regular."

IN SCHOOL CLASSROOMS

Most classroom teachers wonder how they could possibly have the time for one-on-one interaction. However, most of the examples included in this chapter came from weekly conferences that usually lasted from two to five minutes. Many classroom teachers who use a workshop format regularly have short conferences with all the children in their rooms. Sometimes they see all the children weekly, sometimes only every other week. Some teachers see some children weekly and others every other week. The burden of holding conferences is somewhat lightened in the school classroom because there are rarely so many children struggling with reading. Holding conferences is one of the ways that specialists can be integrated into the classroom. When a particular teacher has a number of children who are struggling, the specialist can provide some of the needed one-on-one instruction in conferences.

I would be remiss if I implied that the only direct instruction the children in SRP received occurred in minilessons and conferences. Each child has an afternoon individual tutoring session as well. These sessions, though each is unique depending on the particular needs of the child, follow two basic formats—one for emerging readers and one for those who are beginning to read independently. The sessions for the emergent readers are similar to those that Clay (1993) describes in *Reading Recovery*. They include the rereading of familiar books for comprehension and fluency, the taking of a running record for diagnostic purposes on the book introduced the day before, a minilesson that addresses the child's specific needs, and writing. They close with the introduction of a new book. In addition, twice a week a small group of children and their tutors meet for a sharing session. The sessions for the beginning readers are similar; however, they gradually shift to silent rather than oral reading, and think-alouds take the place of running records.

The tutoring session is a very important part of the SRP children's instruction and is particularly critical for the emergent readers. The one-on-one setting is often the site of very effective direct instruction because it can target the specific situations the child encounters in his or her reading and can be tailored to the child's specific needs. One of the strongest findings in early reading research is that the most effective intervention is one-on-one tutoring. In Vellutino's 1987 *Scientific American* article, he concluded by saying, "We have found that early remediation of reading difficulties is indicated. It should be based on intensive one-on-one tutoring and a balanced reading program" (p. 41). Research reported in *Reading Research Quarterly* (Wasik & Slavin, 1993) indicates schools have recently paid serious attention to this finding. The authors report on five different one-on-one tutoring programs that have been implemented in schools. This model is encouraging, and we need to consider ways to integrate tutoring for students who are not yet capable of reading any text independently.

I am encouraged with new support models that have specialists working with children within the structure of their school classrooms. Models that provide tutoring within the school program show great promise for providing children with the one-on-one help they need without separating them from their classmates and introducing the problems that go along with running several instructional programs simultaneously.

The question of whether children should be pulled out of their classrooms for regularly scheduled tutoring is a difficult one. I think that once children can read some text independently, it is probably not necessary. To read independently a child should be able to read at a late first or early second grade level. If classrooms have available plenty of interesting reading material at an appropriate difficulty level, and if the classroom atmosphere allows children to read at these levels despite their chronological age, I think the support of in-class conferences might suffice.

When children who struggle are slow to reach the late first or early second grade level in their reading, individual tutoring is probably essential. I suggest that this tutoring occur before and after school and in summer programs so that the children's school day is not interrupted and they do not miss out on large segments of classroom activities. Describing the tutoring goes beyond the scope of this book. Suffice it to say that the tutoring must be very good and it must be consistent with the instruction in the classroom.

Direct instruction is an essential and integral part of workshop classrooms. However, children's demonstrated needs—not a set sequence of skills—should prompt the instruction. Because observation of individual children is the foundation of the direct instruction, it accommodates the variability. Carefully scaffolding children's efforts to apply new strategies as they need them to solve problems in their reading and writing is direct instruction at its most effective.

Chapter Seven

Writing Is Indispensable

ON THE first day of the SRP 1989 writing workshop Jimmy and Patrick were sitting by the windows, talking and clowning. They were not writing. I kept stopping by to encourage them to write, and they finally produced two drawings with captions. Jimmy's drawing said, "The dude is a stud." After I urged them more, Jimmy drew a picture of a tree and a boy with a frown and wrote, "I'm bored."

Many of the children at SRP like to write even less than they like to read. Their writing skills, similar to their reading skills, are noticeably less developed than their peers'. However, writing, unlike silent or oral reading, leaves behind a permanent record. Writing documents the children's "deficiencies" in ways they heartily resist. They do not like to have traces of incompetence on paper for all to see. Although the children resist writing, it is an important part of their literacy development. As they attempt to write, they learn about various written forms, which in turn helps them to read those forms when they encounter them. In addition, the act of writing requires phonetic coding and is a natural place for learning the sound-letter correspondences critical to both reading and writing. The children's dislike of writing has been a major influence in the evaluation of the SRP writing workshop.

In SRP 1994 I moved from a writing workshop to a topic workshop. Now the children find a topic and learn about it, and I encourage writing as one of the ways to learn. Both the children and I have been much happier. I am not constantly nagging them to write, and they are able to comfortably and legitimately use forms of expression that take advantage of their strengths—drawing, project construction, and oral presentation.

Issues That Parallel Reading Workshop

Many of the concerns in the writing workshop parallel those of the reading workshop. Choice and motivation are more problematic in writing than in reading. Sharing and direct instruction play significant roles as well.

Choice and Motivation

With struggling writers choice is a big issue. Often their excuse for not writing is that they cannot think of anything to write. The temptation is to step in and tell them what to write. This is not a very effective move. Karen's writing from 1989 is a good example. She wrote two pieces within a week of each other. The first piece (see Figure 4) was the result of lengthy consultation when I bullied her to put something on paper. As nearly as I can decipher the title is "Tall rock hafe," and it reads, "I went to the art museum and I found this and I found it and liked it so I drew it and wrote about it."

She started the second piece, which I call her "Tree Piece" (in Figure 5) on a day when the air conditioner broke and we decided to do writing workshop under a tree. Corrected, it reads as shown at the top of page 87.

Figure 4 Karen's First Piece

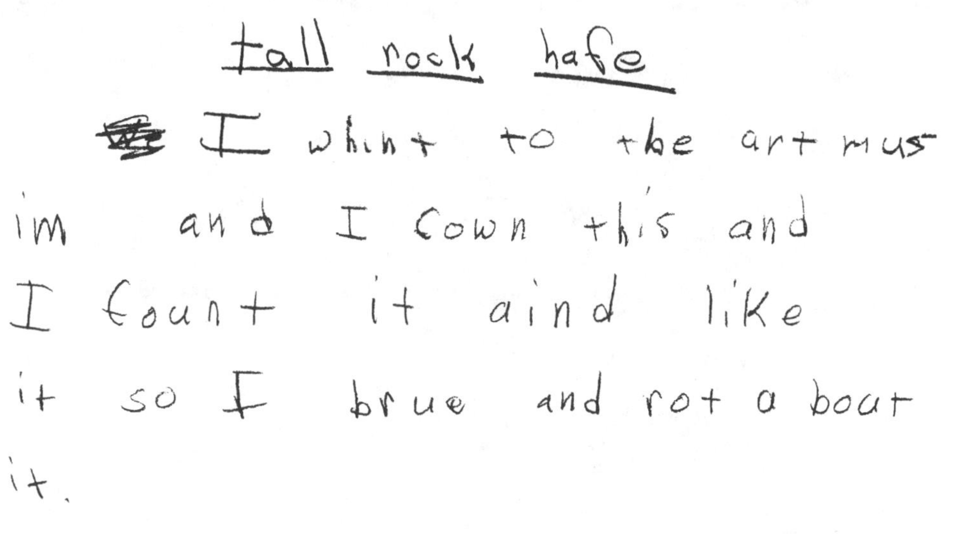
tall rock hafe
I whint to the art mus
im and I cown this and
I fount it aind like
it so I brue and rot a bout
it.

Figure 5   Karen's Tree Piece

The sun   is   brite   and   whorm   and   the
bards   ared   came and   goring   people   walk
from   hear   to   thare. The   treas are   green
and   the   grond hase   grean   grass ard yello and
red   and   outh coulers of folws growing tow,
Now   is   when   almes   look   fore   food   and
people   wark.
And   car   go   bay   and   liatts   Ants
move   a   rown   and   bards   find   them   and
tack   them   to   thary   badys. One, bard
flow   up   rite   be side   me   and it was
a   doy   dird   and   then   a   girl
flow   up   rite   be   sid   him   and
thay   flow a   way, Now   a   bot   the
Ants.   Onw   of   them   corld   on
mag   lage _and I tock it off_   ~~~~ ^Now^ I   had   fun   riteing
this   story   but   I   hoft   to   go   sow see
you   larty.

The   end

The sun is bright and warm and the birds are coming and going. People walk from here to there. The trees are green and the ground has green grass and yellow and red and other colors of flowers growing too. Now is when animals look for food and people work.

And cars go by and little ants move around and birds find them and take them to their babies. One bird flew right beside me and it was a boy bird. And then a girl bird flew up beside him and they flew away.

Now about the ants. One of them crawled on my leg and I took it off. Now I had fun writing this story, but I have to go. So see you later.

I was amazed at what Karen could do once she had something to write that she cared about. Even the handwriting is dramatically different. All the urging in the world could not have produced this piece.

Choice for struggling writers is often limited by lack of competence and the expectation of failure. The entire first summer Jimmy (who wrote "I'm bored") attended SRP, he wrote very little. When he did write, he wrote with a friend. He coauthored a wonderful piece about a pillow fight with Patrick, and he wrote text for several wordless picture books with Sammy. While Jimmy did his share of composing these pieces, he usually let the other child do the actual writing. Although he mostly refused to write, he was proud of these joint accomplishments. On the one occasion when he did initiate his own writing, he drew a picture of his dog's house and wrote, "Taffy is playfyl. bit since." The drawing of the dog house has several unreadable labels and one that reads "Taffy dog house."

During that first summer Jimmy told me lots of stories about Taffy. I constantly urged him to write them down: "Taffy, that's right I remember. Taffy caught the turkey. Did you ever write that story about Taffy?" "Some of it," he replied. I said, "I'd like to—I'd like to hear a whole story about how Taffy caught the turkey. I think that would be interesting." But despite my urging, despite the fact that Jimmy had a topic he cared about, he did not do much writing.

Jimmy returned the next summer a different writer. He wrote an entire book of short stories about Taffy. He wrote them both in writing workshop and in the writing portions of his tutoring sessions (see Figure 6). I think his growing competence and confidence gave him the courage to write. Jimmy came back for a third summer. His longest story of that year was about the motorcycle he received as a reward for good behavior at SRP the year before. The motorcycle story filled a full, typed page. Jimmy's willingness to write grew with his confidence and competence. His love for his dog and his honest desire to share this love helped pull Jimmy into the ranks of writers.

Allowing children real choice is sometimes taxing. One summer James, one of the emergent writers in SRP, produced a poem beginning with the line "Roses are red" as his first effort, which appears at the top of the following page.

Roses are red.
Violets are blue.
Tom is my friend,
And so are you.

I was delighted with the poem and had James teach one of his friends how to write this type of poetry. We also talked about how to write them in sharing. For

Figure 6   Jimmy's Writing

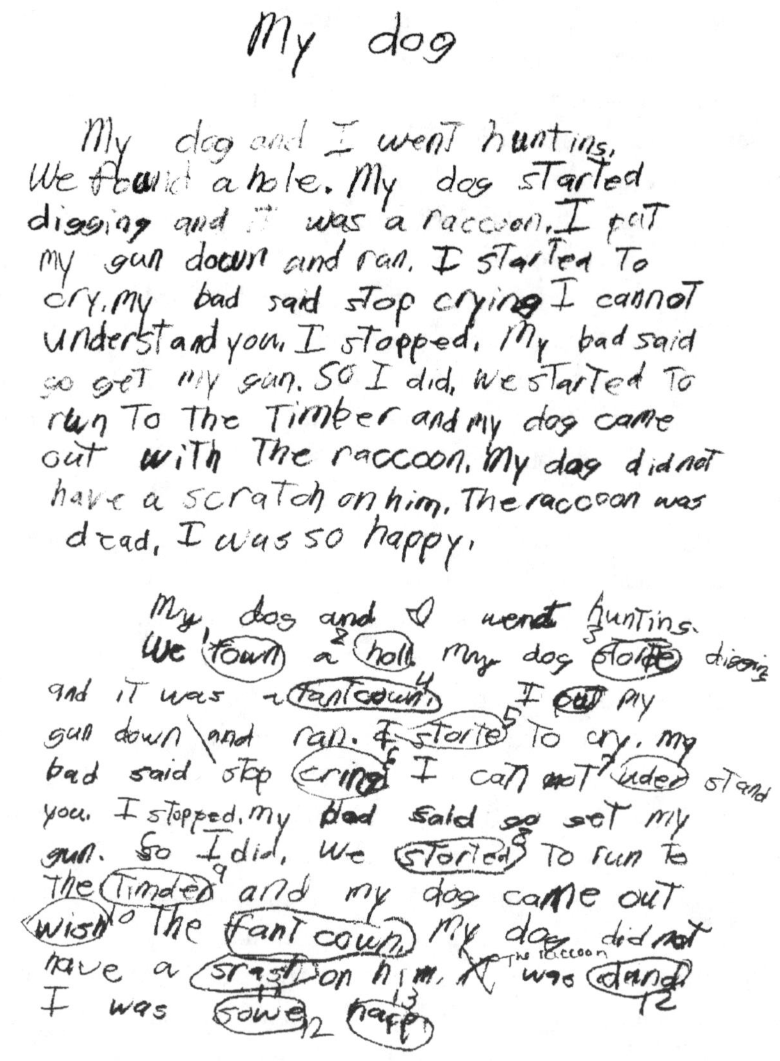

My dog

My dog and I went hunting. We found a hole. My dog started digging and it was a raccoon. I put my gun down and ran. I started to cry. My bad said stop crying I cannot understand you. I stopped. My bad said go get my gun. So I did. We started to run to the timber and my dog came out with the raccoon. My dog did not have a scratch on him. The raccoon was dead. I was so happy.

My dog and I went hunting. We found a hole my dog started digging and it was a raccoon. I put my gun down and ran. I started to cry. My bad said stop crying I can not understand you. I stopped. My bad said go get my gun. So I did. We started to run to the timber and my dog came out with the raccoon. My dog did not have a scratch on him. The raccoon was dead. I was so happy.

days I got "Roses are red" poems—many of them from children who were capable of much more complex writing. I almost laughed the day I received this one:

Roses are red.
Violets are blue.
South America looks
Just like a shoe.

Although I was not sure I was pleased with the students spending time on this type of writing, I thought about the opportunity to teach some map skills with this student and calmed down. I assumed that Milt really meant Italy and took him over to the map. He proceeded to correct me and outlined South America in a way that allowed me to see the shoe. When children have experienced a lot of failure with writing, it takes a lot of persistence and dedication to get them writing. Sometimes the support of a traditional pattern and the interest created by a classroom writing fad gives them the confidence they need to motivate their writing.

As I mentioned, all the urging in the world will not produce the necessary competence and the desire to write. It was because of my constant nagging and the children's paltry writing efforts that I eventually switched to a topic workshop. Originally, in the writing workshop, the children chose topics they were interested in, but they needed more options to express themselves besides through their writing. Because many of them had limited confidence in their writing abilities, they needed to choose a form of expression that took advantage of their strengths rather than focusing on their writing weaknesses. When they can construct projects, draw pictures, and do presentations, they are more likely to become engaged. With encouragement and support they eventually use writing as well.

Sharing

The children's willingness to share their writing belies their unwillingness to write. This willingness shows the power of sharing. Sharing is similar to the readings that authors do on promotional tours. Children like the spotlight. They like to perform before their peers. Because they read their pieces to the group, they do not necessarily have to display the written product.

Most of the writing sharing discussions in SRP focus on the content of the piece. The children often ask questions about content, and the talk is lively because much of the writing contains personal narratives. But occasionally the discussion from these "disabled" children amazes me. For example, when

Karen shared her "Tree Piece" she began by saying, "Um, I'm not quite done with this piece. I've gotten a little about it. It's things that were outside that I've seen so far. About—I don't know. I don't have a title." She then read the piece. One child responded, "Da, da, da, da" (in a rhythmic pattern) and continued to say, "I think it's nice 'cause it's like rhyming—like—like 'the sun is hot' and, uh, like 'the bird is happy' and [uninterpretable]."

The conversation continued in response to another child who asked whether the piece was true, and some other comments were made about being able to imagine just what Karen wrote. Wes questioned Karen carefully about where she got the ideas, and then Karen asked him, "Wes, um, do you like writing poems?" Wes replied, "Poems. I never [wrote] poems before." Then another child asked, "It's sort of like a poem, isn't it?" I answered that it was kind of poetic language, and Karen agreed.

The discussion continued for several minutes, and I called attention to the many pairs in the piece that give it its rhythm. Karen asked if she should read the piece again, and the children encouraged her. The children worked with me to identify and repeat the rhyming pairs. They continued to talk and affirm Karen's capturing of the scenes beneath the tree. Karen concluded the discussion by asking if anyone else had something to share.

Direct Instruction

Direct instruction is as essential in writing as it is in reading, and it functions in much the same way. Usually it begins with a minilesson motivated by something that happened in the classroom. For example, after Karen shared a book she wrote that was based on the pattern of a book she had read, I said,

> What Karen did today, you know, she told you how she took some of the words from the book and she changed some of the words. What we call that is an adaptation of a book by somebody else. And Holly and Erin were telling about the issue of copying books and when you can do it and how, so we'll talk about that sometime tomorrow.

The next day I did a minilesson about quotation marks, and the issue continued to come up throughout the summer with different children. For example, in Chapter One I quoted Erin explaining during sharing her use of quotation marks: "Right here, the part that I read I copied out of the book and I put, um, quotation marks. It doesn't—look right here—but I put his name down here because I wrote what he thinks." On another occasion Wes explained where he found information for his coyote book: "What I did is, um, I looked through *Ranger Rick* [National Wildlife Federation] books, up there, and found some stuff

and then wrote this." At a point in the discussion I asked if he had used quotation marks and he said yes. I reinforced the reason for his use of this punctuation
mark by saying, "To show that it was someone else's words."

ISSUES UNIQUE TO WRITING WORKSHOP

Although writing and reading workshops parallel each other, there are some
special issues in the writing workshop. These include invented spelling, revising,
editing, publishing, using wordless picture books, and drawing.

Invented Spelling

The figures in this book give a fairly accurate picture of the children's invented
spelling and the extent of their reading and writing difficulties. I have noted the
children's extreme reluctance to write. When they come to SRP, many of the
children think of writing as something to be done correctly. Because of the
level of their literacy skills, it is not surprising that they resist writing. If confined to using words that they can spell correctly, they cannot write—certainly
not anything worthy of the thoughts they think. For struggling readers the use
of invented spellings is essential. If we do not allow them wide leeway in their
spelling, convince them that invented spelling is all right to use, and encourage them to use it, they simply will not write.

So often, as teachers and parents, we look at children's creations and see
what they cannot do. We are so shocked by the misspellings that we cannot
see the writing. With younger children we are more tolerant, but as the children
grow older misspellings worry us. We wonder what people will think if they read
something as badly spelled as some of the writing the children produce. Rather
than think of these older children's spellings as something that will develop,
we think of them as something to be remediated. Yet the children's spellings *do*
progress.

Randy's writing progress over three summers is a good demonstration. In
1989, during the first days of SRP, Randy simply sat because he felt there was
nothing he could write. I first attempted to get him to use the printed texts in
the classroom to support his writing. He used a picture dictionary and the book
Round and Round to write his first published book with the same title (see Figure
7). My second goal was to teach Randy to use invented spelling so that he could
write more independently. The breakthrough, which came on Friday of the
second week, was I believe because of a combination of modeling, encourage-

Figure 7   Randy's Writing from 1989

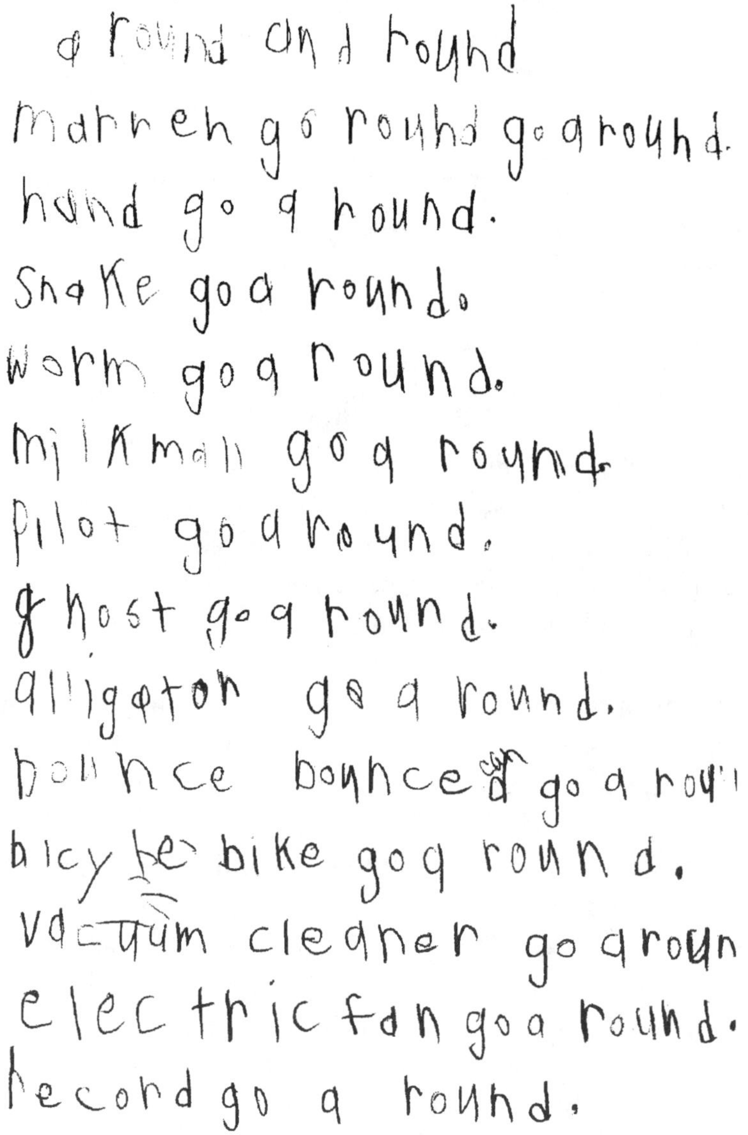

a round and round
marreh go rouhd go around.
hand go a round.
Snake go a round.
worm go a round.
milkman go a round.
pilot go a round.
ghost go a round.
alligator go a round.
bounce bounce go a row'l
bicyke bike go a round.
vacuum cleaner go aroun
electric fan go a round.
record go a round.

ment, and Randy's discovering a topic he wanted to write about, which was suggested by another child. My notes about this breakthrough read as follows:

Wonderful day—He wrote a story about sharks—a shark club—and used invented spelling. Got the idea from Patrick. He wrote 5 or 6 sentences—I have a club called sharks. I have at least 10 people. They wear shark costumes. They drew shark pictures. On costumes he got the c, o, m. Could hear the s and t when I said it.

Figure 8   Randy's Screening Reports

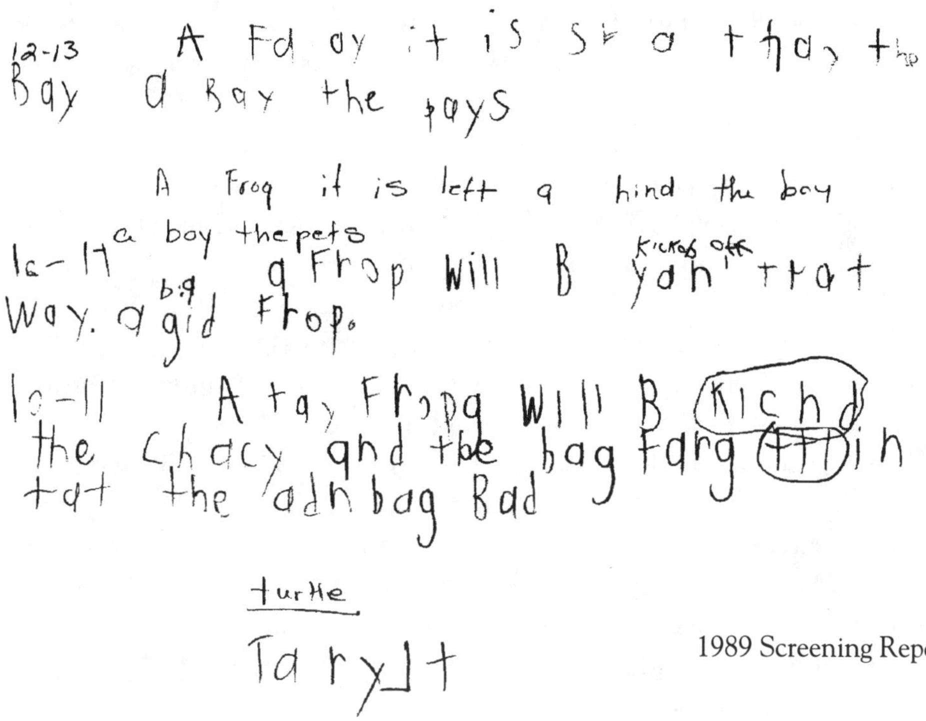

12-13   A Fd oy it is sᵇ a t ʈɑ, tʰᵉ
Bay ɑ Bay the ʈɑyS

A Frog it is left a hind the boy

1ᵉ-1ᵗ a boy the pets
ᵇᵗ qFʈop Will B ʸɑʰⁱ ttɑt
Woy. ɑ gᵗd Fʈop.

1₀-11   A tɑy Fʈɑq WIll B (Kichₐ)
the chɑcy ɑnd the bɑg fɑng (ʈʈ)iʰ
tɑt the ɑdʰ bɑg Bɑd

turtle

Tɑ ry]t

1989 Screening Report

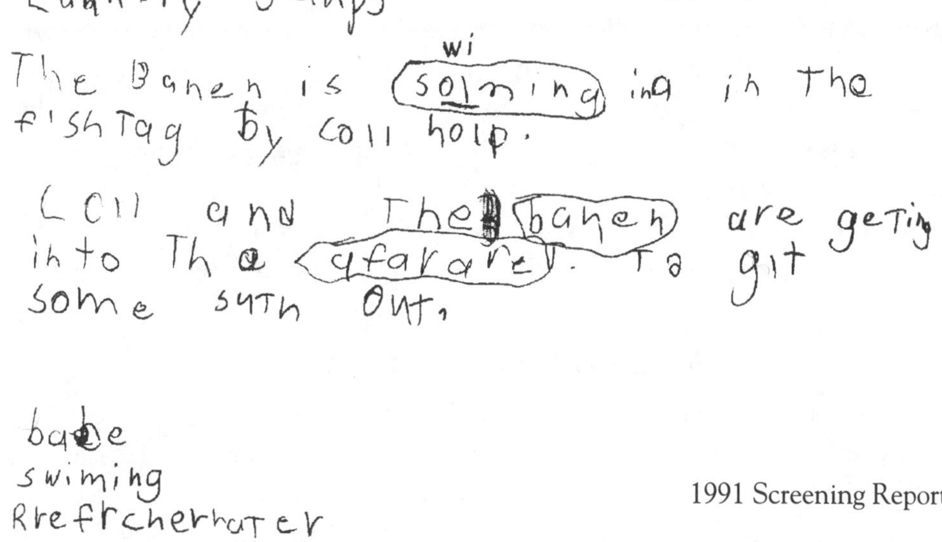

The (Baheₙ) is going boʷn the
LɑunDᵣy. ɑn ᵈ col, run ~~doʷʷ~~ The
~~LɑʰDʈy~~ Sɑnps   ᵗ₀ʷn

The Bɑhₑn is (so|ᵐning) iₐ iʰ the
fishTɑg ᵇy coll hoₗp.

coll ɑnd The (bɑhₑₙ) are geTiₙ
iʰto Tʰₐ (ɑfarareⱼ. Tₐ git
Some SᵤTh ouₜ,

bɑⱸe
swimihg
RᵣefᵣcherhɑTer

1991 Screening Report

93

Figure 8 on the previous page includes writing samples from the diagnostic sessions with Randy that preceeded SRP 1989 and SRP 1991. In both sessions he looked at a wordless picture book and then wrote words to go with selected pages. In the 1989 sample the examiner jotted down what Randy said when he was asked to read only the first sentence of his writing: "A frog it is left a hind the boy. A boy. The pets." The invented spellings do not always have the correct initial sound and do not have final sounds represented. It is difficult to interpret the remainder of the sample. The spelling from the 1991 sample includes considerably more sounds, and to someone familiar with the Karl Series books the sentences are readable: "The baby is going down the laundry and Carl runs down the steps. The baby is swimming in the fish tank by Karl's help. Carl and the baby are getting into the refrigerator to get some stuff to eat." The spelling of "baben" for "baby" includes all the sounds, and "Coll" for "Karl" has both the beginning and endings sounds, as does "soups" for "steps" and "solming" for "swimming." The invented spelling "afarare" for "refrigerator" has the "f" and many of the "r" sounds. Randy's spelling was developing but at such a slow pace that most adults would overlook it. Randy's stories grew in complexity over the three years, and in the final year he produced the Wacky Waters story shown in Figure 9. I am convinced that Randy would have produced very little writing if he had not been afforded the freedom of invented spelling.

We also find invented spelling in the stories of children whose writing is more developed. Often the sound-letter correspondence work that is being done in reading by these children shows up in their writing. For instance, Karen was working on long and short vowel sounds in reading when she wrote her tree piece. In this piece she spelled long sounds variously: for example, brite, grean, trees, green, fore, rite, rite, sid, thay, and riteing. Her growing awareness of the long sounds and how they are produced in writing is reflected in these spellings. Writing is the natural place for the instruction in phonemic awareness and sound-letter correspondences to occur; sounding out is a very natural way to get words on a page. As children write, they practice essential reading skills. I will give an example of this in the next section on revising, editing, and publishing.

Revising, Editing, and Publishing

When I work with practicum students and inservice teachers, the topic of revision always comes up. They tell me they cannot get the children to revise. I, too, have trouble getting children to revise. Usually, I am so glad when the children write anything at all, that I do not push revision. My few successes with revision have come when a child shared a piece during writing sharing and other chil-

Figure 9   Randy's 1991 Wacky Waters Story

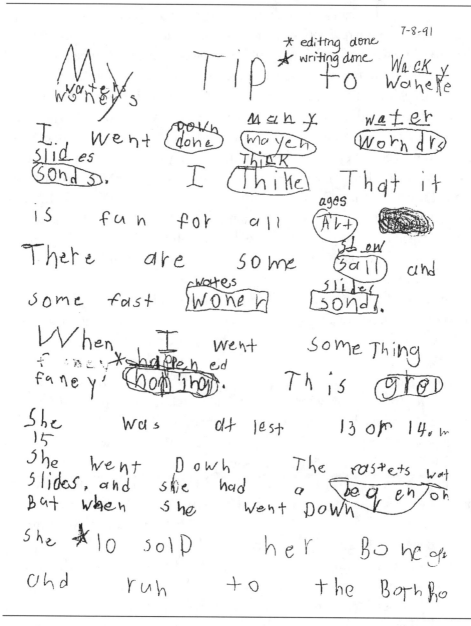

dren asked questions because information they were interested in was not in the piece. I know that for me revision is sometimes a chore, but it is a real audience such as the one I envision for this book that has sustained me during the laborious revision process. Friends' responses to drafts of my manuscript have helped me see the places where I am unclear or disorganized or where I left out something important. I think if I taught the children in SRP for more than 5½ weeks at a time I would press for more revision, but I do not because it is very important to move these struggling writers forward to a published piece that they can be proud of. If they are reluctant to revise, I simply move on to editing and publishing.

For struggling writers, editing by others is essential. If older children's final products are confined to what they can produce alone with errors, they will produce nothing because others will sometimes ridicule them. At SRP we encourage children to edit their own work as much as they can. But often the editing task is monumental: a single piece may include as many as 40 unconventionally spelled words. In the case of many invented spellings, we might ask the child to correct five that are particularly appropriate, and then we would correct the rest as we typed it on the computer for publishing. It is important for students to see high-quality, correct, attractive versions of their writing, which can also motivate more writing.

The editing session also provides good opportunities for some of the sound-letter correspondence teaching that is necessary. The children can often identify the unconventionally spelled words in their drafts. For example, in his Wacky Waters story, Randy was able to circle many of his misspelled words after his tutor taught him an editing procedure. Randy would say the circled word and listen for the beginning sound. He would check it and correct the first letter if necessary. Then he would say the word again slowly and carefully, this time listening for the ending sound. Again he would write this down. He then said the word a third time, listening for the sounds in the middle of the word. Eventually he was able to pronounce each circled word slowly and carefully, running his fingers under the letters he had written to see if had actually written all the sounds he pronounced. During this process Randy was developing the phonemic awareness critical for reading.

Another important aspect of the writing of this piece was that Linda Fielding (who was teaching the classroom that summer) edited with Randy daily, small amounts at a time, so that Randy still remembered the content of what he had written and could read it back. There were some false starts on this piece when too much drafting was done before any editing and neither Linda nor Randy could read enough of the work to edit it. Several other children we have worked with require frequent editing in contrast to more skilled writers for whom early editing may interrupt the writing process.

Revising, editing, and publishing are not only about correct spelling. Lessons also focus on elaborating ideas, using concrete details, sequencing ideas effectively, using story maps to brainstorm, and so forth. Randy found that using story maps allowed him to move from producing short half-page stories to multipage efforts. In his second summer he used a story map to produce a lengthy story titled "Mystery at SRP."

Wordless Picture Books

Creating stories for wordless picture books has been a very successful activity at SRP. We give the children pads of small, sticky notes on which they write text. Then they stick the text on each corresponding page of the book. We photocopy the book and type the children's text on the appropriate page. On the cover we give the original title and author and then write the students' name. Figure 10 on page 98 is an example of the sticky notes Jimmy and Sammy created for their "Dune Buggy" story based on *Dune Bug* by J.A. Raabe.

Often the children work together on these books and really enjoy themselves. I think they are successful because the pictures reduce the complexity of the task. With the story in the pictures, they can add a few words and produce a creditable text. I found this was a good way to start, and then in minilessons I encouraged them to add more to their text. For example, in one minilesson, I said the following:

> One of the things I've noticed, particularly in the, uh, Mercer Mayer books, is that during sharing time, we can't see the pictures well enough. So a lot of times we don't understand the stories. And one of the things, one of what you did, was you let us know what was happening in the story line. And that was a good thing to do in sharing.
>
> Another thing you could do is put more of the story in your words, couldn't you? Most of you are just sort of giving, saying, saying what the character says. But you could also tell the story as well as just adding what the characters say. And then when you came to sharing, 'cause the story was in the words, when you read it to the class, they would be able to understand it. So that's something to think on.

Drawing and Other Expressive Forms

The first several writing workshops of SRP made me very nervous. I think part of the reason was that I knew less about writing than I did reading and was less confident and knowledgeable about the writing process. The children did not want to write, but many of them are good artists. They like to draw and make projects. In 1989 several children worked on a farm project. They used construction paper to make a three-dimensional model of a farm. It took many days, and we do not have very many days with the children in the summer. It also involved several children, and they were not writing. How were they going to

Figure 10   Example of Text for a Wordless Picture Book

will pop over a hill with
d Dune Buggy

Then will filled his
dune Buggy with gas

Then will went to a repar
shop and got a Tun up

Then will went to sleep on
d rock

Then Alex stole will Dune
Buggy

Then Alexs drove in the
water

will called the police

and Then Aalxs got cot
caught

learn to write if they did not write? I told them they could only do projects if they wrote about them. When they said they were not done with the model because they needed more horses, I responded, "Not until I see stories, let me tell you." The children complained, "You saw stories!" Later as I was explaining who had written about the model, the children squabbled about who else had to write about it because they had worked on it.

The next several summers I had fewer art materials displayed in the classroom and only brought them out as specific children requested them to go along with their writing. However, as long as there were paper, pencils, markers, and crayons in the room, the children drew. Finally, in 1994 I decided to stop fighting the children about creating art. My colleague, art educator Steve Thunder-McQuire, was instrumental in this decision. As part of a teacher inservice sessions he talked about how he sometimes lets children write stories in order to get them to draw and how he worries about the fact that they spend so much time writing. How will they learn to draw if they do not draw? Both are about creative expression and they often work together. I now let the children make projects, invite a class of college students in on the last day of SRP to watch the children's presentations, and encourage writing when it seems appropriate. I try to keep Jimmy in mind, whom I mentioned at the beginning of this chapter, and remember that 5½ weeks is a very short time. Often the children are producing what they can with the limited skills and limited confidence they have. Working with struggling writers requires great trust and patience.

RECIPROCAL INFLUENCES OF READING AND WRITING

Including writing workshop in the literacy instruction of struggling readers is important because reading and writing constantly influence each other. The act of writing provides opportunities for learning the sound-letter relationships that help reading. Knowing a sound-letter relationship in reading can help in writing. Wanting to write an informational story can encourage a child to read informational books. Reading books can spawn the desire to write books like them. When children share the books they have written it means they read them.

Jimmy's collection of stories about his dog Taffy is a primary example of how reading and writing are intertwined. At the end of Jimmy's first summer, he discovered the old Dolch book *Dog Pals*, part of a series that has hardbound but plain covers and few pictures. They are very easy texts with highly controlled vocabulary, but they look like chapter books for older students. Jimmy was thrilled that he could read them. He spent all the reading workshop time engrossed in them and carried them back and forth to the dorm until he finished them. He even read them while standing in lines. His classmates started calling him a bookworm. His book about Taffy, written during the second summer, used the same format as the Dolch book (see Figure 6).

Several children in SRP have been strongly interested in reading informational books, which has influenced their writing. I mentioned Susan and her shark book in Chapter Four. Mary was fascinated by kangaroos. I gave her many books about kangaroos and she spent hours reading them. Figure 11 is an early draft of her own kangaroo book.

I think Karen's tree piece, which I talked about earlier, was also strongly influenced by her reading. In her tutoring session, she read the book *Deer at the*

Figure 11   Mary's Book About Kangaroos

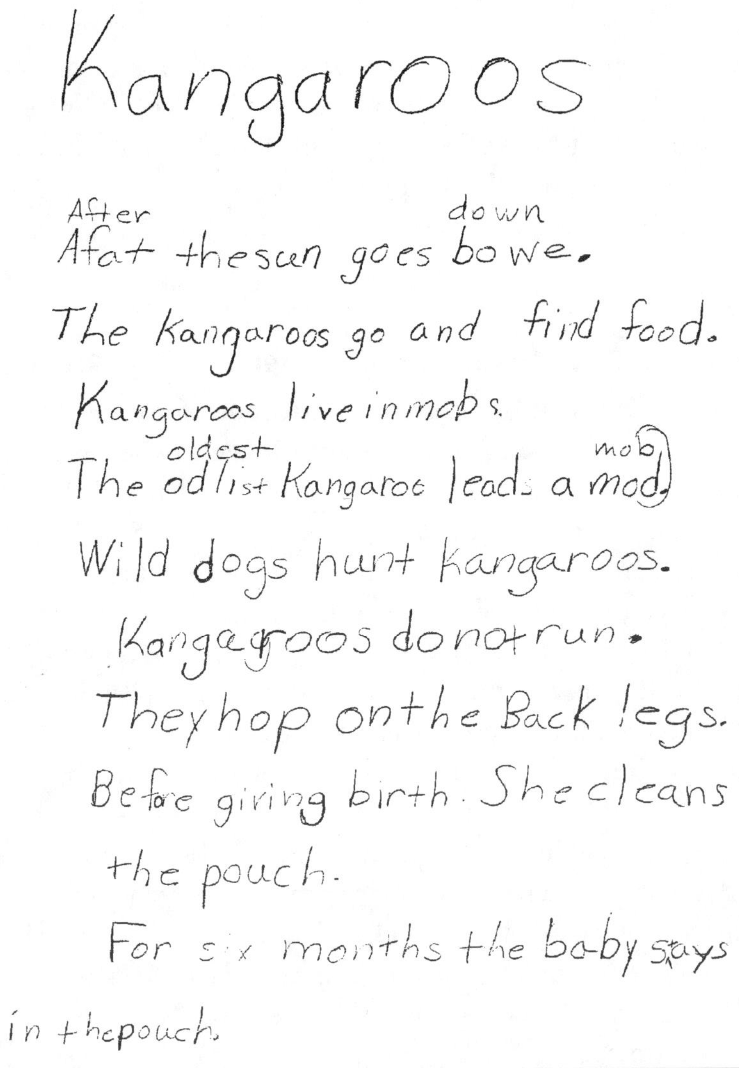

Kangaroos

Afat thesun goes bowe.
(After ... down)

The Kangaroos go and find food.

Kangaroos live in mobs.

The odlist Kangaroe leads a mod.
(oldest ... mob)

Wild dogs hunt kangaroos.

Kangaroos do not run.

They hop on the Back legs.

Before giving birth. She cleans
the pouch.

For six months the baby says
in thepouch.

Brook by Jim Arnosky. It is a beautiful book with wonderful illustrations and lyrical language. Karen read it many times until she could almost recite it. Karen's tutor encouraged her to write an adaptation of the book called *Horses at the Brook*. Here is what Karen said when she shared this adaptation:

> OK. I kinda took the book called the *Deer at the Brook* and I took it and copied some words down, and I made some words up of my own instead of *Deer at the Brook*, I called it horse...um...*Horse at the Brook*.

Then she read:

> The brook is a good place. The brook is a good place. Sunlight on the water. Water on the stones. The brook is a place where horses go to. Some together, some come alone. Mothers bring their babies. Watch the fish. Watch the fish. They run and play on the sandy bay and nap in the sun. Sunlight on the sparkle, sparkle on the water, water on the stones. The brook is a sparkling place.

As she finished a child remarked, "It kinda sounds like a poem." Although I cannot directly trace the language from *Deer at the Brook* to Karen's tree piece, I think her love of this book, her multiple rereadings of it in a lyrical style, and her use of it in the *Horses* adaptation probably contributed to the lyrical quality of her writing in this piece.

Karen's adaptation is quite sophisticated, but patterned books can offer children whose skills are less developed an entry into writing when nothing else can. As I mentioned earlier, Randy's first published book used the pattern of a Wright Story Box Series book.

IN SCHOOL CLASSROOMS

The most important message for the regular school classroom is that struggling readers need a lot of support in writing. Often, with good reason, they are extremely reluctant writers. The level of work they can produce on their own is simply unacceptable to them and to their teachers, parents, and peers. Classrooms that have a regular procedure for editing and publishing must be able to provide a high level of editing support for these children. This is not to say that they should be excused from writing and editing; they cannot learn to write and edit if they do not write and edit. But expectations should be realistic and invented spellings must be tolerated in draft writing. Editing support is critical so that struggling writers can produce products that are worthy of respect. With this in mind, trained parent volunteers and aides can be useful as editors for struggling readers and writers in school classrooms.

In addition, alternative forms of expression must be allowed. In the 1994 SRP a group of boys was working on a project about mummies. The boys had tried to exclude Ralph from working with them, and he was in tears. I intervened and insisted he be included. The boys reluctantly tolerated Ralph. When the boys decided that they needed a jeweled dagger to bury with their mummy, Ralph volunteered. He was an excellent artist and produced a magnificent dagger complete with sequins for jewels. (The sequins were provided by Charlene Hall, a graduate assistant who worked in the room that year.) From that point on he was a member of the group. Just prior to the final presentations for the college student audience, he wrote a caption to identify the dagger. His drawing skills gained him acceptance and in the end inspired some writing.

Writing is a partner to reading and an integral part of learning language. The fact that I have devoted only one chapter to writing should not be interpreted to mean that writing is not important. I organized the book this way because there is a lot written about writing already and because the parallel nature of reading and writing workshops often makes writing about both redundant. But writing is essential to struggling readers' literacy development. Struggling readers, although they are often reluctant writers as well, can benefit from full participation in a writing or topic workshop. In school classrooms, where the variability is even wider than at SRP, this is a special challenge. The most difficult obstacle is creating an environment where all of the children's efforts are respected and nurtured. The respectful and nurturing atmosphere of the workshop is the foundation on which all the children's growth depends.

Chapter Eight

Observation and Record Keeping Guide Learning

E **ARLY IN** the first week of SRP 1989, I finished the day and I realized that I did not know what Jason had done that day. My first thought was, "It's a good thing I don't have a principal to walk in here and say, 'How did Jason do today?'" I would have answered, "Fine," and that would have been fairly accurate. The fact that I did not know what he was doing probably meant that he was doing what he was supposed to be doing, but it has taken my focused attention through four years of SRP to develop a system of record keeping that makes me feel competent to answer the question, "How's _____ doing?" I started with a clipboard with cards for each child taped on it, but it was awkward, and I kept setting it aside and losing track of it as I moved. The next thing I tried was taking notes on 8½" x 11" paper that I filed in a three-ring notebook. That did not work because I kept losing the notes before I got them filed in the notebook. What I have settled on is a 5½" x 8" spiral notebook that fits in my jacket pocket, a binder that has pocket folders for forms and for each child, and a set of forms. Armed with these materials I can keep track of all the children in the classroom.

The most important thing I have learned through my record-keeping system is that planning becomes evaluation in the workshop classroom. Let me explain. When I was teaching with more traditional methods, I had to develop specific lessons around specific stories—sometimes three lessons or more for a single day. In contrast, in my workshop classroom children choose what they read on a daily basis. I cannot plan lessons about a story because I do not know what the stories will be. Instead, each day I know that I will be working with several children. Instead of planning lessons that focus on stories, I review children's records and think about them. I think about what I know about each child, what kinds of books each child is reading, what kinds of strategies each is using, and I decide if there is anything in particular that I want to address when I meet with each child. So my planning time is evaluation time—looking over children's records and thinking about the children, what they are doing, and what I might expect from them next. This planning time helps me know the children well enough to run a child-centered workshop classroom.

THE MECHANICS OF RECORD KEEPING

My record-keeping system has eight basic components as follows:

1. a Daily Log form
2. two sticky pieces of note paper
3. a 5½″ x 8″ spiral notebook
4. children's Reading Logs
5. children's reading and writing folders
6. a large binder with pocket files
7. a final report form
8. a portfolio for each child

In the sections that follow I describe each element of my record-keeping system. The figures are replicas of actual sample notes from SRP 1994 with pseudonyms substituted for children's names.

Daily Log and Reminder Notes

I use a Daily Log form both to plan the day and later to summarize it. Figure 12 is my daily log for the second day of SRP 1994. To the left of the bold line I remind myself of what I want to do, and to the right I record what actually happened. For example, during group talk the left side indicates I wanted to talk about reading difficulties with the children. The right side shows that several of the children got into a dispute about whether cars turn over when they hit trees, and then we talked about the dorm activities. Each morning, based on the left side of the log, I prepare two notes to stick on my spiral notebook, which serve as reminders (see Figure 13). The large note reminds me of the focus of each of the day's activities, and the small one lists the children I want to hold conferences with that day.

Figure 12   SRP Morning Classroom 1994 Daily Log

date 6/21/94

Talk about reading

Group Talk
Not much talk about reading. Jackson, Carl, Timmy and Jackson in a dispute about whether cars turn over when they hit trees. Talked about activities.

~~Better~~
Skip the Goal form and work on the log

Reading Workshop
went well — Jackson taking a long time to get started — Used the rug today
Jackson A and Jackson D doing some dream books - but did read

Emphasize they must have a book ready to share.

Sharing (Small Group)

| Allie }
Mandy } | Jackson }
Jackson }
Carl | Jeff }
Dante }
Samuel } | Chose own groups.
Worked well |
| Brook }
Linda }
Sally } | Robby }
Timmy }
Ralph } | | |

Encourage all the children.

Sharing (Large Group)
Dante and Jeff   Mike Fink
Jackson B   Our Street
Carl   Last
Jackson A   A ZOO "stupid cause it doesn't have all the animals

Recess

"Pardon", Said the Giraffe Chp. 2. Tawny

Oral Literature
"Pardon" Said the Giraffe
Ants Like Picnics, too
up to party Chp. 3 in Tawny

Encourage them to continue learning about their topic

Topic Workshop

| Robby }
Ralph }
Timmy } Space | Carl }
Jackson A }
Jackson B } | DIRT
BIKES
CARS | Dante & Mandy - KWL
D.D. reports Brook editing and instructing Sally
Girls seem pretty productive
Except Mandy and Allie at a loss. |

Skip Goal Sheet an focus on Recording in Log

Sharing (Small Group)
Several kids wanted to share - we did it in large group.

Figure 13   Daily Reminder Notes

G.T - Reading
R.W - monitor Jackson and Timmy for really reading
OL   Pardon, Said the Giraffe Get from Sally
T.W Allie and Mandy - try to help Ralph find something he can read about space

6/21
Ralph
Robby
Allie
Linda

Spiral Notebook

The notebook is a standard spiral that fits in my jacket pocket, is perforated so that the pages tear out easily and without a mess, and allows completed notes to be turned to the back leaving a fresh flat surface for notetaking. I use the spiral to take three kinds of notes: general class notes, conference notes, and sharing notes. Figure 14 presents examples of each. In the general class notes example, down the left side I was keeping track of where children were located and with whom they were working. The circled groups indicate the small groups that the children sorted themselves into for discussion. I used these notes to fill in the log sheet in Figure 12.

My conference notes are an important element of the record-keeping system. In conferences I learn most about the children and their reading. My notes for emergent and beginning readers almost always include a running record—a system developed by Clay (1993) to record exactly what children say as they are reading a text. For each word a child correctly pronounces I make a stroke, and when the child departs from the text, I write down what he or she says. I draw a line underneath the child's words and write the actual text word below the line. From this record I glean critical information about the child's accuracy levels and strategies. The conference notes for Allie are included in Figure 14. She read *If You Meet a Dragon* by Joy Cowley with 100 percent meaningful accuracy, and she self-corrected when she read "nose" for the text word "toes." My notes indicate I think she can read more difficult material and suggest trying the I Can Read Series with her.

My sharing notes are probably unintelligible to any one but me. I record the title of the book, the essence of what the child shares and the questions that other children ask. I try to write as many key words as I can, and usually this is enough to remind me of the session. The example in Figure 14 shows my notes for Jackson's sharing of *Our Street* by Joy Cowley. They indicate that he compared the houses to other people's houses and showed bigger, smaller, skinny, and tall houses. He said one house was like a tent and one was like a motor home. The children asked if there was anything about dog houses in the book and if the last house was brick. Another child asked who wrote the book, and another commented that the whole book talked about houses.

Children's Reading Logs and Folders

Figure 15, on page 109, is a sample of the children's Reading Log form. The children use this form to keep a record of what they read. The logs for 1994 had spaces for the title and date, a line for comments, and a space to record the num-

Figure 14 Spiral Notebook Notes

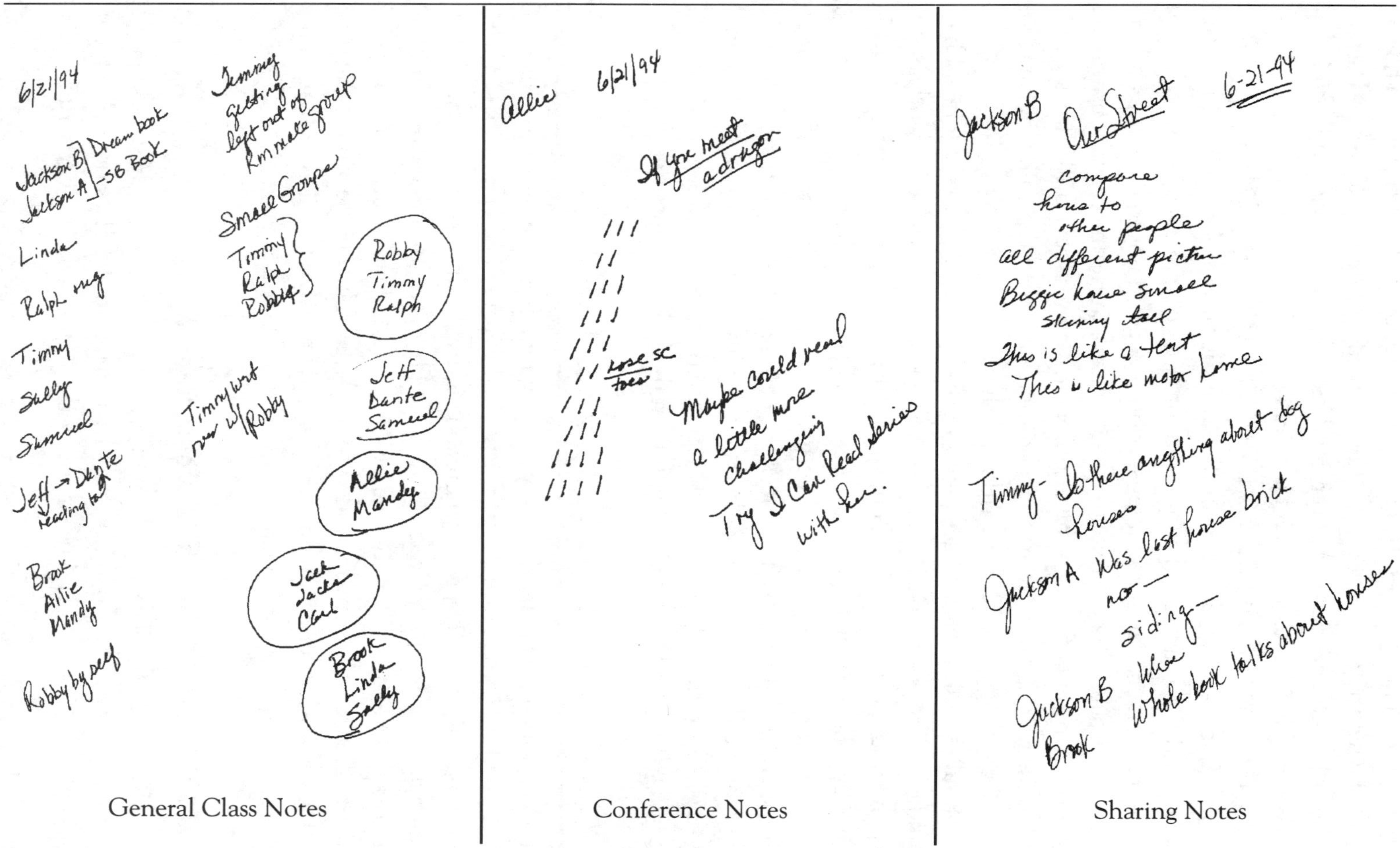

General Class Notes   Conference Notes   Sharing Notes bers of the strategies (listed on the bottom of the page) they used. The log serves two purposes. First, it gives the children a sense of accomplishment. They are proud of what they have done, and they are pleased to ask me for a new log form as they fill each one. Second, it is a good record for me to refer to when I want to see what kinds of books a child is reading.

The idea of having children write comments and record strategies on their Reading Log was a good one, I think, but it did not work for 1994. I find that every year I try and then abandon one or two good form ideas, which I will talk about in more detail in a later section. I decided not to have the children fill in the "thoughts" and "strategies used" parts of the form because this was taking too much time. Some of the children write with great difficulty, so minimizing the writing on the forms makes sense. For most of the children, I am happy if they manage to fill out the title and the date.

It takes a lot of effort to get some of the children to fill in the forms. I have found over the years that I need to take the last few minutes of workshop to stop, remind the children to fill out the forms, and then monitor them to make sure they follow through. At times, even though I am reluctant to use external motivators, I have given the children stickers for filling out their logs. Until the routine is established, I need to check the children's folders every night to make sure they are filled in. For those that are not I leave "see me" notes on the folders to get the forms filled in properly. The children keep their logs in their reading and writing folders, which they store in their plastic containers.

Pocket Binder

I use a two-inch pocket binder as my filing system. It is a simple three-ring notebook that I fill with pockets. I use the pockets because I can put things in without snapping open the rings. My notebook is divided into several sections. Several pockets are for memos relating to SRP. There are several pockets for blank forms, and I have a pocket for each week where I file my daily logs along with the general class notes and reminders for each day. The final section of the notebook has a pocket for each child. At the end of each day I file the sharing and conference session notes about each child in that child's pocket.

Classroom Report

The SRP Morning Classroom Report, or final report, is the best summary of what guides my record keeping and observation in the classroom (see Figure 16 on pages 111 and 112). I use many of the notes I take daily to write this re-

Figure 15   The Children's Reading Log

Name _____

Title	date
pages read thoughts	strategies used

Title	date
pages read thoughts	strategies used

Title	date
pages read thoughts	strategies used

Title	date
pages read thoughts	strategies used

Title	date
pages read thoughts	strategies used

Title	date
pages read thoughts	strategies used

Strategies 1. reads ahead to solve problems   2. rereads to solve problems   3. uses meaning and pictures to help with words   4. checks letters and sounds to help with words   5. figures out word meanings   6. relates to own life 7. predicts   8. relates to other books   9. retells/summarizes   10. other

port for each child. It reflects the four important general goals I have for the children, which I mentioned in Chapter Two. The first is that they understand the importance of reading to learning to read. I read excerpts from Stanovich's (1986) article on Matthew effects and write on the chalkboard the number of words that low, average, and high readers in the first and fifth grades read during a year. I want the children to understand that one of the major differences between good and struggling readers is that good readers read a lot more words than do struggling readers. This goal is represented by the paragraph that begins the "comments" section of the report.

As mentioned earlier, in addition to reading many words there are three other things that I think the children must be able to do to become readers: (1) choose good books, (2) use good strategies, and (3) make reading make sense. These are listed after "Reading Workshop" with brief descriptions of actions that I look for as evidence. They are also listed in the descriptive paragraph that begins the "comments" section. I like these categories because they are general enough to be flexible. For example, choosing good books may mean choosing simple, repetitive texts for one child, whereas it may mean choosing transitional chapter books for another or informational articles for another. The uses good strategies category can focus on the particular strategies each child needs to develop—making a word-print match for emergent readers, reading on to aid word identification for beginning readers, or using personal experiences to make sense of what happens in a book for developing readers. For each descriptive activity I refer to my notes and my memory to decide whether the child does something almost always, sometimes, rarely. I complete this part of the report by writing a description of the child's reading behaviors and reading progress. The other side of the form is devoted to the "Topic Workshop" and is similarly organized.

Portfolios

Several times I have attempted to have the children construct portfolios. I felt that using a portfolio would be a good way for the children to document progress for both themselves and others, such as parents and teachers at their home schools. My attempts, however, have not been particularly successful. I give each child a small folder with pockets and tell the children they can put whatever they want in them. Almost all of them fill their pockets with their Reading Logs or other lists of vacation, just right, and dream books, and they often include a tape of themselves reading. However, I am disappointed in the lack of variety in the portfolios. I wish the children would find ways to represent their

Figure 16 SRP Morning Classroom Final Report

Name_____

Rating Scale: A=Almost Always   S=Sometimes   R=Rarely

Reading Workshop

Chooses good books

____ initiates own reading

____ chooses vacation (easy), just right, and dream (too hard) books with confidence

____ spends almost all of workshop time really reading

Uses good strategies

____ reads ahead to solve problems   ____ relates to own life

____ rereads to solve problems   ____ makes predictions

____ uses meaning and pictures to help with words   ____ relates to other books

____ checks letters and sounds to help with words   ____ retells/summarizes

____ figures out word meanings

Makes reading make sense

____ talks about books with classmates

____ explains books well to the teacher

____ explains books well during sharing

____ raises and explains problems and confusions

Comments

In the summer classroom the students learn that they can do things that will help them learn to read. We emphasize that students who read well read many words and that those who read less well read fewer words. Researchers estimate that the number of words fourth to fifth grade students read per year ranges from 100,000 for less able readers to nearly 50,000,000 for avid readers. In addition, the children have learned three things they must do: (1) choose good books, (2) use good strategies, and (3) make reading make sense. Choosing good books means a child is choosing books where he or she can read most (90%) words correctly. If a child can read most words he or she can usually figure out the rest by using good strategies. The children have also learned that they must always make their reading make sense.

_____

_____

_____

_____

(continued)

_____

Figure 16 SRP Morning Classroom Final Report (cont'd)

Topic Workshop

Chooses good topics

_____ chooses topic independently

_____ chooses appropriate topic with confidence

_____ spends almost all of workshop time really learning

Uses good strategies

_____ identifies and locates information sources

_____ plans for final product

_____ prepares initial drafts fluently

_____ uses good organization

_____ rereads and reviews for sense

_____ uses readable temporary spelling

_____ revises for content

_____ edits for mechanics

_____ presents final product well

Makes topic make sense

_____ talks about topic with classmates

_____ explains topic well to the teacher

_____ explains topic well during sharing

_____ raises and explains problems and confusions

Procedures

_____ talks during group talk

_____ listens and participates in oral literature

_____ reads during reading workshop

_____ studies during topic workshop

_____ fills out record forms

_____ responds to others during sharing

reading strategies and other important things they have learned. But 5½ weeks is a very short time to accumulate much documentation. I do not introduce the portfolios until the end of the fourth week, and the children simply do not have much time to devote to them. So, I have to make the choice between spending the time reading or spending the time documenting it. Although I continue to use portfolios I remain unsatisfied with the way I have implemented them. Portfolios will continue to be a development focus for me.

I continue to be hopeful about porfolios because of some work that Sylvia Forsyth, a graduate assistant who was involved in SRP 1992, did with the records from that SRP. She used a combination of copies of items from the children's portfolios and from my records to construct portfolios for use in a research study (Forsyth, 1993). She shared these with two teachers who had no knowledge of the children prior to seeing the portfolios. She found that the teachers could use the portfolios to estimate children's reading abilities accurately, and the teachers commented that the portfolios were very informative. The portfolios gave them a good idea of where to begin instruction with the children.

Abandoned Forms

As I noted earlier, every year I create and abandon several forms. As an example, Figure 17 is a Small-Group Log form. It was an attempt to get children involved in setting their own goals and monitoring their own performance. Although this is important, the form was not helping the children. It was taking so

Figure 17 Small-Group Log

Date_____

Names   Goals

1. _____

2. _____

3. _____

4. _____

	set goals	made progress	completed log	responded	shared
1.	_____	_____	_____	_____	
2.	_____	_____	_____	_____	
3.	_____	_____	_____	_____	
4.	_____	_____	_____	_____	

much time to explain and fill in the forms that little real goal setting and monitoring were going on. I have still not solved the problem of children's goal setting, and I continue to focus on that. I always find myself wishing for more time with the children because I am sure, if we had it, we could get them involved in the goal setting. As for monitoring the small groups, the form is not necessary. With children meeting in groups of threes and fours at desks around the periphery of the classroom, I can stand on the central rug and monitor the groups fairly well. I have also found that the groups do not need much monitoring because the children like to bring a book for small-group sharing and talk about it. I include this abandoned form here as a record of the trial-and-error process I have used to build my record-keeping system.

USING THE RECORD-KEEPING SYSTEM

To show how the system works I have chosen three children at different levels of development—Manny, an emergent reader; Tommie, a beginning reader; and Emma, a more advanced reader. The examples show how various record-keeping components contribute to my developing characterization of each child as a reader.

Manny—an Emergent Reader

At midterm, I evaluated Manny's progress in three areas—choosing good books, using good strategies, and making reading make sense (see Figure 18). Manny knew how to choose appropriate books, but did not like the books. However, when he shared, he always shared appropriate books. My notes indicate that I was not yet sure of his strategies and suspected that there were gaps in his sound-letter relationship knowledge. He preferred meaning cues to print cues and made sense when he shared. I was concerned about Manny because he had complained that he was the worst reader and writer in the class (although he was not) and that he could not find books that he could both read and enjoy.

These evaluations were based on my memory of interactions with Manny and on conference notes from June 22nd, 23rd, 30th, and July 7th, as shown in Figure 18. On the first day of SRP, June 22nd, Manny came to me and said there were not any books that he could read. I helped him find some Story Box Series books by Joy Cowley and taught him to read *Danger!* On the 23rd I had a formal conference with him and took a running record on a book he had read before. My notes indicate that he first said "kittens" for "cats," then he correct-

Figure 18   Notes on Manny—an Emergent Reader

Manny   7-13-92   Mid-Term Evaluation

A. Choosing Good Books

1. Manny knows what he can read but doesn't like these books

2. Shows appropriate Books

B. Using Good Strategies

1. Can't evaluate too well - seems not to be making word/print match - but pointing helps

2. Sometimes doesn't know sound associated w/letter making some progress

3. ~~Anticipating~~

C. Make it Make Sense

1. Using Meaning nec print cues

2. Shows appropriate ileg

Concerns

Manny complains that he's the worst reader/writer
Can't find books he can read that he likes
I need to evaluate word/print match and use of initial and final consonant sounds.
He wrote Dragon Story - and some prose - but often doesn't use letter sounds in writing - sometimes doesn't know, as in _ch_

6-__-92

Manny
Couldn't find book he could read
I helped him with SB book
Danger - Told him to practice

Manny   Cats ✓✓
         Kittens Txt

                  ✓✓✓
                  ✓✓✓
                  ✓✓✓

23 }   ✓✓✓
                ✓✓✓
                ✓✓✓

Any new words today   behind - talked about this

Horace - trouble w/Horace

Manny is finding books

(continued)

Figure 18   Notes on Manny—an Emergent Reader (cont'd)

ed himself and I said that the word "kittens" would be too long. We talked about how he was learning new words, and he read *Horace* but had a lot of trouble with it. My final comment was that he was finding appropriate books.

The next week I took a running record on *The Bee*, another Story Box book. He read with almost 100 percent accuracy and made two self-corrections. I commented that he was using his finger to make a word-print match. He had misread "out the flower" instead of "out of the flower," and when he noticed he had a word left over, he went back and self-corrected. I also noted that I worked on ending sounds with him.

In the third conference I had a list of concerns at the top of the page—selection, word-print match, pointing, initial consonant, final consonant, pictures, meaning, and skipping. Manny read two books for me, *If You Meet a Dragon* by Joy Cowley and *The Bike Lesson* by the Berenstains. He read *Dragon* with 100 percent accuracy and was considerably below acceptable levels on *The Bike Lesson*. My notes say "selection sketchy—Story Box OK—*Bike Lesson* too hard." I also noted that he was making a word-print match on *Dragon* but not *Bike Lesson*, and I "couldn't observe strategies—*Dragon* too easy, *Bike Lesson* too hard." The themes that run through the conference—concerns about book selection, making a word-print match, and using initial and final consonants—formed the basis of the midterm report. I had two more conferences with Manny before I wrote his final report. These are my comments on his final report:

> Manny is in the beginning stages of learning to read. He knows how to choose just right books [misses 2 or fewer words in 20] but is sometimes discouraged because he doesn't like the topics of many JR books.
>
> Manny can use good strategies when he is reading JR books. He points to monitor whether what he is saying matches the print. For example, in the story box book *The Bee*, he read the line "out of the flower" as "out the flower." He realized that there was a word left over and went back to read the line correctly. We have also taught Manny to use the sense of the book and look at the letters to help with words he doesn't know. For example, in *The Bike Lesson* he had difficulty with the word "before." I encouraged him to finish the page and then think about what was happening in the story. He then reread and looked at the letters and identified the word as "before." When I asked how he got the word, he said he didn't know. But when I said I thought he might have looked at the "b-e" and thought "be," he said he had noticed "for." Manny has good strategies but lacks confidence in them and needs much encouragement to use them.

In my daily notetaking I try to focus on choosing books, using strategies, and making sense, three of the goals I mentioned in Chapter One and earlier in this chapter. These three categories emerged over successive SRPs because they were predominant issues for many of the children. As I take notes I try to jot down specific examples, as well as general statements, so that when I write a report I can provide concrete evidence to both support and illustrate the general claims.

Tommie—a Beginning Reader

Tommie's midterm report was short and succinct:

1. Tommie can choose good books.

2. Sometimes relies too much on sounding out and not enough on meaning.

3. Sometimes focusing at a fairly literal level—need to move to some higher level thinking.

This midterm report was based on three conferences that occurred on June 24th and 29th and July 9th (see Figure 19). During the first conference Tommie read *Sheep in a Jeep* by Nancy Shaw for me, and several times he stopped for long periods trying to sound out words. I worked with him at length on using meaning to help his word identification. My running record indicates that the book was at an appropriate level. I also noted that Tommie was having difficulty using rhyming cues and that he was doing some self-correcting. I have a cryptic note to myself that says, "What am I learning?" that refers to our conversation about what he was learning. I asked him to try to do some of the things we had done together when he was reading: "Read ahead, think about the meaning. The meaning really helped you." I used my running record to point out places where he had used these strategies while reading to me.

His next conference was quite brief because he was immersed in *Here Comes the Strike Out* by Leonard Kessler. I did a brief running record, noted that the book was a good choice, and let him read. In the July 9th conference I talked with Tommie about his progress in the three areas and asked him to report on what he was doing. My notes indicate that he was reading a book about pigs, and he read *Thomas' Snowsuit* by Robert Munsch for me. I also note that I was worried about Tommie's feelings about just right books. My notes on Tommie's final report follow:

> Tommie has read many books this summer. He understands that he should choose just right books [misses only 2 words in 20] that he likes. However, it is sometimes difficult for him to do this. Many books that might be just right for him are on topics that he is not interested in. For example, Tommie read *This is [the] Bear* [Hayes] because he knew the words but he thought the book was kind of stupid. However, he found several good JR books: *Here Comes the Strike Out* and *Tim's Dog Muffy* [an unpublished personal book] were two that he especially liked.

Figure 19   Notes on Tommie—a Beginning Reader

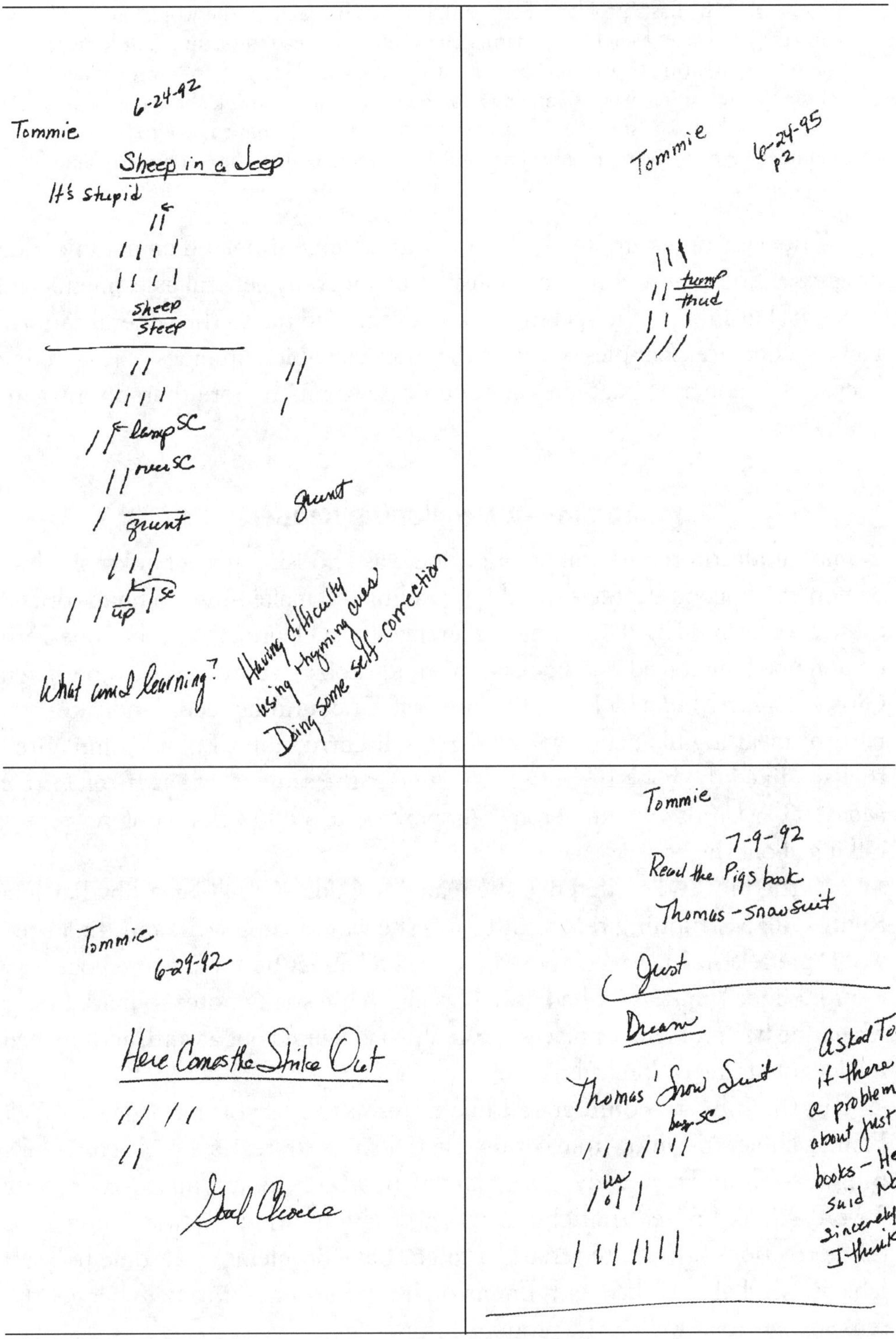

Tommie   6-24-92

Sheep in a Jeep

It's stupid

|| |
/ / / |
/ / / |

sheep / sleep

/ /
/ / / |
/ / lamp SC
/ / ruu SC
/ grunt   grunt
/ / /
/ / / up / SC

What am I learning?   Having difficulty using rhyming cues)   Doing some self-correction

---

Tommie   6-24-95 p2

/ / /
/ / turnip / thud
/ / /
/ / /

Tommie   6-29-92

Here Comes the Strike Out

/ / / /
/ /

Goal Choice

Tommie   7-9-92

Read the Pigs book
Thomas - snowsuit

Quest

Dream

Thomas' Snow Suit
beg SC
/ / / / / / /
/ / us o /
/ / / / / / /

Asked Tommie if there was a problem— about just right books— He said No— sincerely I think

Tommie uses good strategies when he is reading just right books. He knows what to do when he has a problem. For example when he came to the word "pretend" in *Song and Dance Man* [Ackerman], he read ahead, reread, thought about letters, and then identified "pretend" because it made sense. This was an improvement from the beginning of the summer when I had to ask him to think about the meaning to get the word "steep" in *Sheep in a Jeep*. Sometimes Tommie needs to be be reminded to make the text make sense and not spend too much time trying to sound things out.

The daily notes are invaluable in both documenting and communicating progress. I find that without the notes I remember my general assessments and concerns but I forget the specific instances that led me to the generalizations. Having concrete examples is one of the most valuable outcomes of notetaking because the concrete examples communicate so much more than do the generalizations.

Emma—a Developing Reader

Emma's midterm report was strong. She was choosing good books, she had demonstrated good strategies, and her reading did make sense to her. I formed these conclusions based on three conferences (see Figure 20). In the June 25th conference Emma read two books to me and I took a running record on *If You Give a Moose a Muffin* by Laura J. Numeroff. The running record indicates 100 percent meaningful accuracy with three self-corrections. Emma commented that she liked the book because it had almost the same words as *If You Give a Mouse a Cookie* also by Numeroff. We spent quite a bit of that conference just talking about the books.

In the July 2nd conference she read *The Candy Corn Contest* by Patricia Reilly Giff. My running record indicates she was reading well, and the jotted word "pretzels" refers to a conversation we had about how she figured out how to pronounce "pretzels." I had asked Emma to use sticky notes to mark places where she had problems or places where she had figured out a word, and she had used a note to mark "pretzels."

In the July 7th conference I had notes at the top of the page to check Emma's choice, meaning from context, and flexible strategies. I took a brief running record on *The Candy Corn Contest* in which Emma miscued on only 2 words of 20. I noted that choice was all right and that she was doing good self-corrections. I indicated that she might have problems with some polysyllabic words. I also worked with Emma on using the context to help her get the sense of a word as well as the pronunciation.

The notes from Emma's final classroom report follow on page 122.

Figure 20 Notes on Emma—a Developing Reader

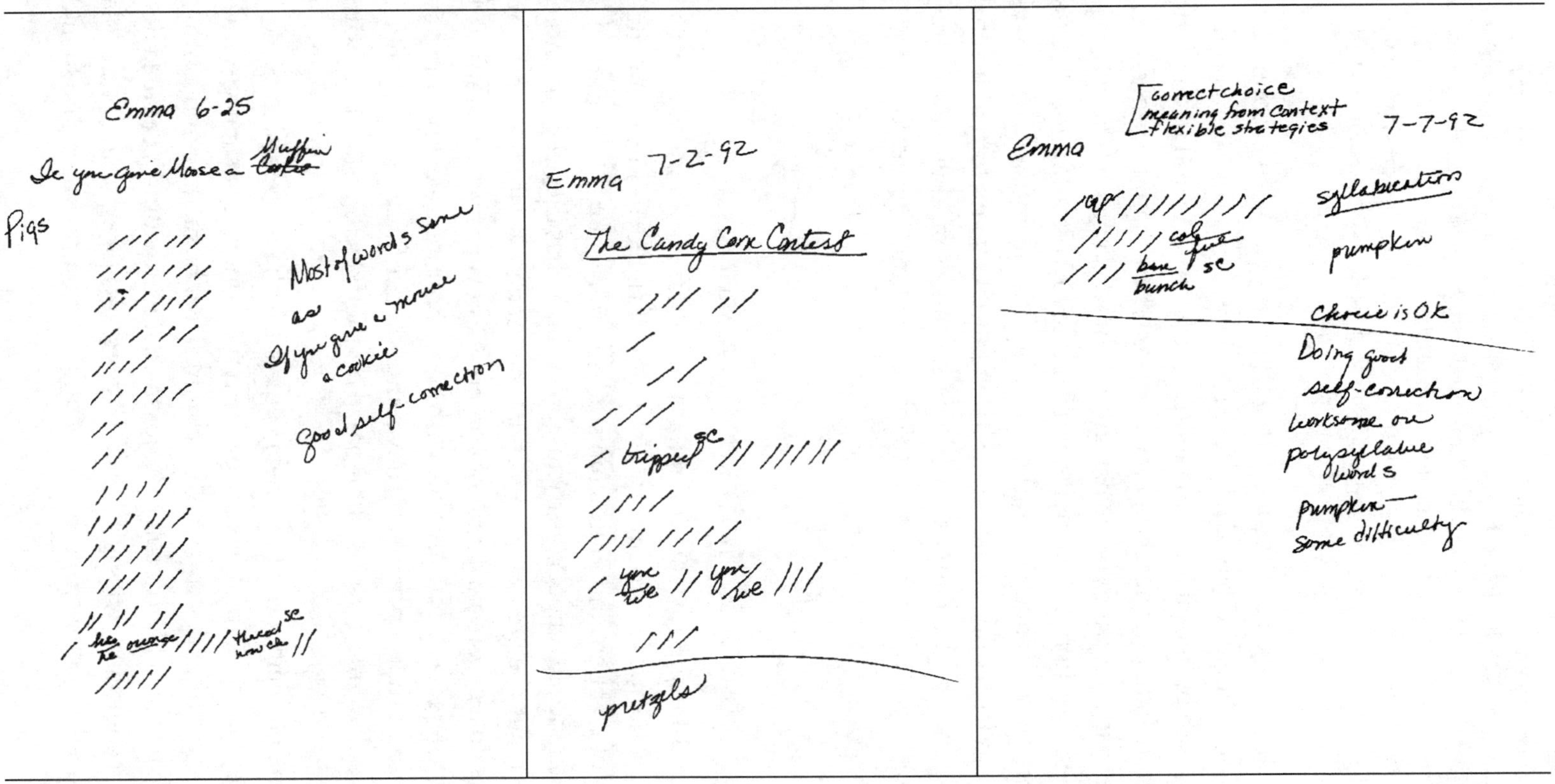

Emma has reached the stage of independence in reading. She knows how to choose good books and can find books that she both can read and wants to read. She has particularly enjoyed books by Patricia Reilly Giff this summer. Emma uses good strategies when she reads. For example, when she was reading a book with her tutor, she encountered the word "soprano." She didn't know it but she read on, reread, thought about the meaning and used the letters, and she identified the word correctly. Emma knows that the key to her future progress in reading is to select just right books (books in which she struggles with no more than 2 words in 20), to use her strategies, and to focus on making sense.

I felt very good about Emma that summer. It was her second summer with us and she seemed to have "got it." She spent the entire summer immersed in reading both by herself and with another little girl who also liked Patricia Reilly Giff. I notice that my notes on Emma are sketchier than the others, and my conferences with her were somewhat shorter. In fact, when it came to report writing time I was short on examples and went to her tutor for one. Because Emma was working well independently, I paid her less attention than I paid to children I was less confident about. Although we have no formal mechanism for tracking the children after they leave us, Emma's mother called after the first reporting period of seventh grade to tell us that Emma received all high marks in her classes.

IN SCHOOL CLASSROOMS

My record-keeping system is similar to the systems I have seen operating in regular workshop classrooms. In fact many of the ideas I use came from observations of teachers and practicum students in regular elementary classrooms. One difference in school classrooms, however, is that they contain more than 15 children, but the greater numbers can be accommodated several ways. Some teachers do a classroom round of conferences every two weeks instead of each week. Others have conferences with some children weekly, some every two weeks, and others only when they request a conference. These teachers pay differential attention to children based on their needs just as I did with Emma, Tommie, and Manny.

One problem school teachers confront is the weekly plan book. How are they supposed to turn in weekly plans to the principal or supervisor when they do not know from day to day what children will be reading and writing? Several of the teachers I know solve this problem by providing a detailed description of how reading and writing workshops work at the beginning of the plan book. If they need a substitute teacher, they indicate that the substitute should refer to the description at the beginning of the plan book on each week's entry. In the daily squares they note which children they plan to see and a few major concerns or questions for each child.

Another difference I would expect in school classrooms is that teachers may take fewer running records. They are only necessary at the very early stages of reading development and when children are consistently making inappropriate book choices. Also, conference notes for more developed readers, such as Samuel in the SRP classroom, may focus on other issues such as solving comprehension problems and getting vocabulary meanings from context (see Figure 21).

Final reports might also be less individualized in a school classroom. Although the individualization is the point of workshop instruction, and teachers should try to individualize reporting as much as they can, time constraints may dictate more standard reporting. When classrooms are organized around a set of goals that most children are achieving, the standard part of the report can be expanded and the individualized notes made briefer except for those children whose performance is distinctly different.

There are several ways in which I hope record-keeping systems in regular classrooms would go beyond the one I have described here. As the failed Small-Group Log form attests, I am eager to have children set their own goals and self-evaluate. I am confident that if they are given more than 5½ weeks chil-

Figure 21   Conference Notes on Samuel—a More Developed Reader

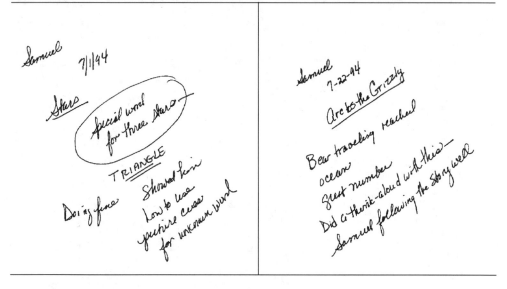

dren can do this. I have seen children in regular classrooms take a strong and active role in the evaluation of their own progress. I have observed systems that allow children to collect notes and artifacts related to their reading development and use these to evaluate themselves. In several classrooms, children do their own evaluation presentations at parent-teacher conferences. In addition, I think portfolios could be very effective in promoting the kind of self-evaluation that I would like to see.

Good record keeping is absolutely essential to a workshop classroom. If a teacher cannot remember what the children do from day to day—and no normal human being can—he or she cannot get to know the children very well. The point of a workshop classroom for me is to accommodate the variability and uniqueness of each child. A good record-keeping system makes this goal a reality.

Chapter Nine

What Does This Mean for Schools?

T HE CHILDREN I have worked with who are described in this book did learn. In most school settings, however, their learning would be overlooked because it is measured against what other children can do. In the SRP children's regular schools, most children continue to learn to read at faster rates than they do; and even as the SRP children gain, they are left further behind. Their gains in reading are hard earned, but they do not count for much in the day-to-day life of a traditional school setting. Because in schools the focus is on grade levels and normal and average achievement, growth that leaves the children still behind their peers is discounted. Children whose learning is not recognized and respected are likely to quit on us; in fact, children like those we see in SRP regularly drop out of school.

Current patterns of instructional organization do not serve struggling readers well. Our schools and classrooms do not adapt well to many kinds of differences, including linguistic, racial, cultural, and socioeconomic differences—any type of variability. We know a lot about how children learn to read, and we know that there is wide variability in the rate and manner of literacy learning. Acting on this knowledge means reorganizing the delivery of literacy instruction. There are ways to teach literacy that accommodate the reality of variability and allow children the dignity of learning at their own rate and in their own ways.

THE CHILDREN IN SRP LEARNED

For several years I administered the reading tests (level 7, forms G and H) of the Iowa Tests of Basic Skills at the beginning and end of SRP. I used the level 7 tests, designed for first and second grade children, because I wanted to be sure that all the children could read the tests. I used raw scores rather than any of the available standardized scores because the interpretation of these scores for the SRP children is somewhat problematic. I used the tests even though I knew the short-term (5½ weeks) intervention was unlikely to show much effect on the children's reading scores. The standard error of measurement on the test in grade-equivalent terms was longer than the 5½ weeks of instruction in SRP. The children I was working with had failed to learn to read despite several years of instruction; it was not reasonable to expect them to make up for years in a few weeks. There was statistically significant growth for the children as a group only once, and I did not trust the result. The child who showed the most dramatic improvement in scores did not read either the test passages or the items; he simply colored in the ovals on the answer sheet without referring to the test.

However, for most of the children who attended SRP in 1989 (not the year for which there were statistically significant effects), I have ITBS scores for each summer they attended and can look at the scores over a span of one or two years. I am not claiming that any growth or lack of growth can be attributed to SRP. The scores cover a time period in which the children received instruction at school in regular and special education school classrooms and in SRP in the classroom, small-group, and individual tutoring sessions. In addition, some of the children's parents read to them and worked with them regularly. It is impossible to trace effects to any particular instructional setting.

Figure 22 The Children's Gains in Grade-Equivalent Scores from ITBS (Level 7)

| | Years gain | | | | |
	-1	0	+1	+2	+3
1 summer		2			
2 summers	1	2	2*	2	
3 summers		2	2	2	

Length of time in SRP

*An entry score for one of these children was not available because the child was scheduled for tutoring at the test time. I have estimated her entry level based on the initial screening and performance during the first week of SRP.

126

Figure 22 displays these scores. The shaded diagonal of the chart represents expected growth in reading achievement for all children—a year's growth in a year's time. The two children who fall above the shaded area made accelerated progress—that is, they grew more than a year in a year's time. Six of the children fall on the diagonal, indicating that children who had failed to make expected progress in learning to read until they entered SRP did make expected progress following their participation. Figure 23 on the next page shows samples of typical text these eight children could read upon exiting SRP. Six of the eight were reading text similar to that in *Alice and the Birthday Giant* by John F. Green, and the other two were reading text similar to that in William Steig's *Doctor DeSoto*.

Of the seven children who fall below the diagonal in Figure 22, five demonstrated substantial growth in the complexity of the text they could read as they exited SRP. On the informal reading inventory that we administer in the screening session, all five were reading below the primer level (as shown in the text of Pamela Allen's book *Who Sank the Boat?* in Figure 24 on page 129), regardless of whether they had completed second, third, or fourth grade. When they exited, one child could read text as difficult as that in *Alice and the Birthday Giant* in Figure 23, and four children could read text as difficult as that in the following passage from Patricia Reilly Giff's book *Ronald Morgan Goes to Bat*:

> I pulled on my red and white shirt,
> the one that says GO TEAM GO
> and ran outside to the field.
> "Two things," Mr. Spano told us.
> "Try hard, and keep your eye on the ball."

Even the informal inventories do not detect an increase in reading ability for the two remaining children. Neither could read comfortably at the preprimer level after two and three summers at SRP. However, there was noticeable growth in their literacy knowledge that is best illustrated through writing samples. These two children came to us at age 10 with very little understanding of the mechanics of written language. Although both knew many consonant sounds, and both had had extensive phonics instruction, they did not seem to understand the relationship between spoken and printed language. For example, one of them wrote, "Well he got a pest and he send I wanrn is." He read this back as, "Well, he got a present and he said, 'I wonder what is in it.'"

In both this student's reading and writing the number of words he read or wrote often did not correspond to what he said. Two years later in another writing sample, there was a one-to-one correspondence with his spoken lan-

Figure 23   Text Samples from Children's Books

Alice's father had decorated the kitchen with balloons and ribbons. The table was covered with paper plates, pointed hats and horns, hot dogs, pickles, and ice cream —and lots of presents.

Alice's mother was carrying in the biggest, most scrumptious looking chocolate birthday cake any of them had ever seen when they heard the sound of thumping footsteps. Everybody stopped having fun to listen.

From *Alice and the Birthday Giant*, text by John F. Green (1990). Illustrated by Maryann Kovalski. Reprinted by permission of Scholastic Canada, Ltd., Richmond Hill, Ontario.

After office hours, Mrs. De Soto molded a tooth of pure gold and polished it. "Raw with salt, indeed," mumbled Doctor De Soto. "How foolish to trust a fox!"

"He didn't know what he was saying," said Mrs. De Soto. "Why should he harm us? We're helping him."
"Because he's a fox!" said Doctor De Soto. "They're wicked, wicked creatures."

That night the De Soto lay awake worrying. "Should we let him in tomorrow?" Mrs. De Soto wondered.
"Once I start a job," said the dentist firmly, "I finish it. My father was the same way."
"But we must do something to protect ourselves," said his wife. They talked and talked until they formed a plan. "I think it will work," said Doctor De Soto. A minute later he was snoring.

From *Doctor DeSoto* by William Steig. Text and illustrations copyright 1982 by William Steig. Reprinted by permission of Farrar, Straus & Giroux, Inc.

Figure 24   Sample of Text at the Primer Level

Was it the sheep
who knew where to sit
to level the boat
so that she could knit?

No, it wasn't the sheep
who knew where to sit.

Do you know who sank the boat?

From *Who Sank the Boat?* by Pamela Allen (1983). Published by Coward-McCann, Inc. Reprinted by permission of Curtis Brown (Aust) Pty Ltd., Sydney.

guage. He wrote, "The Babe is iting in the fis dol," and he read, "The baby is getting in the fish bowl." The one-to-one correspondence was consistent throughout the writing sample.

The other child's writing growth was similar. A typescript of one of his initial stories follows:

> The gann Bar
> Gane Bulls gan
> rane. gann tane. To my
> oyo Caane nanen the
> ganndane. sean men.
> nen Dadn. Pane eat the gann bear.

He read the story like this:

The Gummy Bear

A gummy bear was driving in gummy car. He got a phone call on his gummy phone. A person said, "Come right over." And he did. He knocked on the gummy door. The person said, "Come in." The person ate the gummy bear up.

Figure 25 on the next page shows the first draft with initial editing of a story about sharks this child wrote a year later. The story displays a one-to-one correspondence between spoken word and print.

Figure 25   A Child's Writing Sample Displaying One-to-One Correspondence Between Spoken Word and Print

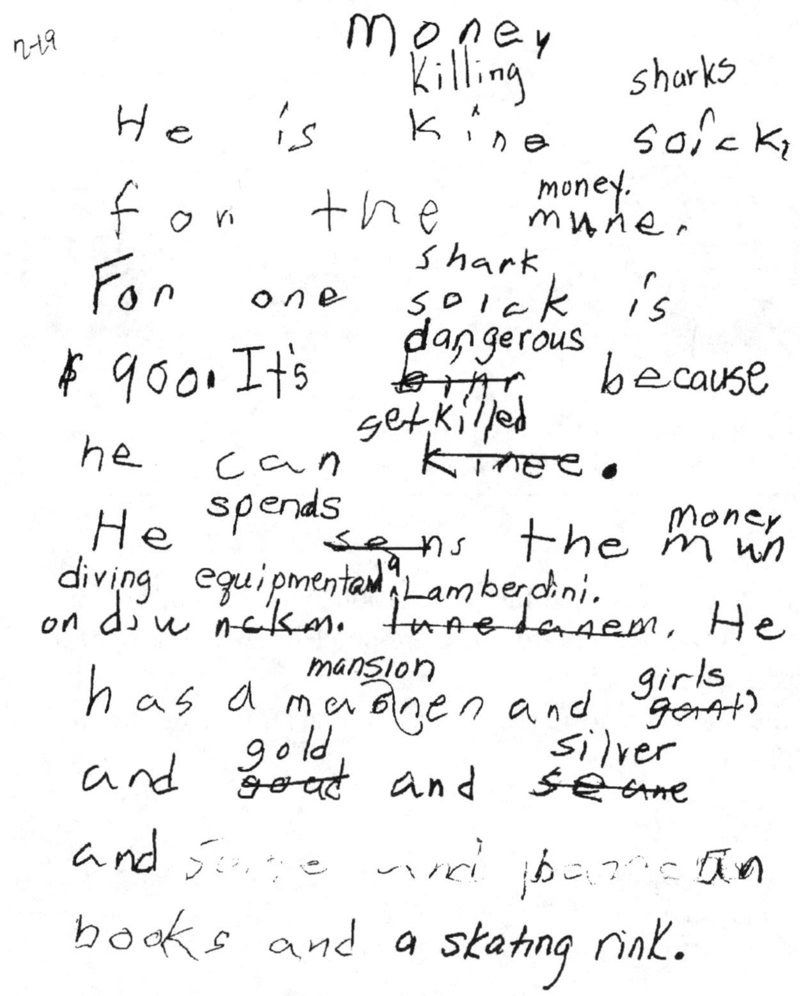

He read the story:

He is killing sharks for the money. For one shark is $900. It's dangerous because he can get killed. He spends the money on diving equipment and a Lamberghini. He has a mansion and girls and gold and silver and books and a skating rink.

Over the years they were involved in SRP all the children grew in their literacy knowledge. Most of them made detectable growth on a standardized instrument (administered out of level). Two actually made accelerated growth!

Some made detectable growth on informal reading inventories, and the growth for two children was most apparent in writing samples collected over a long period. All the children learned.

UNRECOGNIZED GROWTH

The SRP children's growth was probably not recognized at their regular schools for several reasons. One reason is that very rarely do we look at the text children can actually read as an indicator of progress. Although most of the 1989 SRP children attending for at least two summers could read more difficult material when they exited than they could when they entered, many of them could not read texts that were appropriate for their grade levels. The fall after their final SRP summer, all the children who attended SRP 1989 were entering at least fourth grade. However, the text contained in a typical fourth grade reader is considerably more difficult than any of the texts the SRP children could read. Some of the SRP children entered seventh grade after their final summer at SRP. So, although they all grew and some made accelerated progress (grew more than a year in a year's time), these children's peers were still ahead of them in literacy development, and the SRP children could not read grade-level texts. I do not mean to imply that all the children were forced to read grade-level texts. Many of the schools adapted the children's instructional programs so that they were able to read more realistic texts. But it was clear to everyone that they were not reading what all the other children could read.

Another reason that the children's growth was not recognized at their schools was that they rarely improved on their school-administered standardized tests. This is not surprising. I administered the ITBS first and second grade test to the SRP children regardless of their grade level in school. When the school gives them grade-level tests, they cannot read them. So from year to year, the tests show that they cannot read. Although it is possible to use out-of-level testing that will detect the children's growth, this is rarely done.

If we looked at the children as a group, we might also conclude that they have not grown much. For the children attending two summers, the mean raw score on the ITBS increased 10 items from 33 to 43. For the norm group 33 was the score achieved by children who were in the first grade, seventh month. The 43 was the score achieved by children who were in the second grade, third month. So in terms of the norm group, the SRP children grew about six months. For those attending three summers, the scores are similar with grade equivalent advancing from 1.6 to 2.3. The children's standardized scores advanced, on the average, six to seven months over the span of years (one or two) they attended SRP. (These scores, as IRA resolutions indicate, should not be interpreted to mean that the children read at a particular absolute grade level; the texts presented earlier in the figures are more accurate indicators of the text that children could read.)

I am reluctant to report such scores. Six or seven months of literacy growth seems like so little gain for so much time and effort. Programs are dismantled for gains better than these. And yet I want to argue strongly that the children did grow. Our inability to recognize that growth is the crux of the problem in teaching these children to read.

The children's skills improved noticeably, if you look at the products of their work and use tests appropriate to their abilities, such as out-of-level standardized tests or informal reading inventories. However, if you look at standardized scores and normed performance from grade-level tests, the improvement is often negligible and frequently does not register. This is not to say that there is anything inherently wrong with standardized tests. They probably give us an accurate measure of what these children can do compared with others their age, and there is a place for such information. Standardized tests are not created to demonstrate the growth that children at the bottom of the distribution make. They are created to tell us who is at the bottom of the distribution, who is in the middle, and who is at the top. Once we have that information we need to move beyond standardized testing and the mentality that surrounds it.

The point is that comparison to others their age is beside the point with these children. We already know that they cannot do many things that their same-age peers can do. We do not need to know how bad they are and what they cannot do. We already know that and so do they. What we do need to know and what the children (and their teachers and parents) need to know is what they can do and how they are growing. Samples representing the growing complexity of the text these children can handle and writing samples such as the ones presented in this book are good concrete ways to demonstrate children's growth over time. Tape recordings of reading are also dramatic, and analyses of running records can be helpful as well.

The children we work with at SRP are struggling to learn to read. Many of them have received special help, even before-school intervention. They are struggling to learn to read for a variety of reasons, most of which we really do not understand. Although inappropriate instruction contributes to their difficulties, it is seldom the sole cause of them. But still our instructional goals must be more realistic. We should aim at teaching every child to read and write as quickly as it is possible for *that child* to learn to read and write. We need to ask, given a particular child with a particular performance and behavior in my class, what is a likely next step and how can the child and I work together to make that goal a reality? Rather than be upset that children like the SRP children are three, four, and five years behind their peers, we should calmly and matter-of-factly acknowledge that some children learn to read quickly and easily, whereas others learn slowly and with great difficulty. Children should not be penalized, punished, or humiliated because of the way they learn to read and write.

We Need New Organizational Patterns

Many current organizational patterns of instruction *do* penalize and humiliate students. They are predicated on the false assumption that all children of the same age learn literacy skills the same way and at the same pace. They do not. We know that. Some children learn to read and write before they come to school. Others, like the SRP children, struggle with each small advance.

When children fall behind their age-mates, they are relegated to pull-out remedial and special education programs. The pull-out programs segregate the children from their peers and stigmatize them, as mentioned earlier. The children in these programs tell many stories. For example, Jason wrote me the letter that appears in Figure 26. The translation is "Dear Dr. Roller, I felt different from other kids. People were mean to me and called me different from other kids. I have only three true friends." Of the three children he named two were other SRP children (with whom he interacted only 5½ weeks of the year).

Figure 26 Jason's Letter

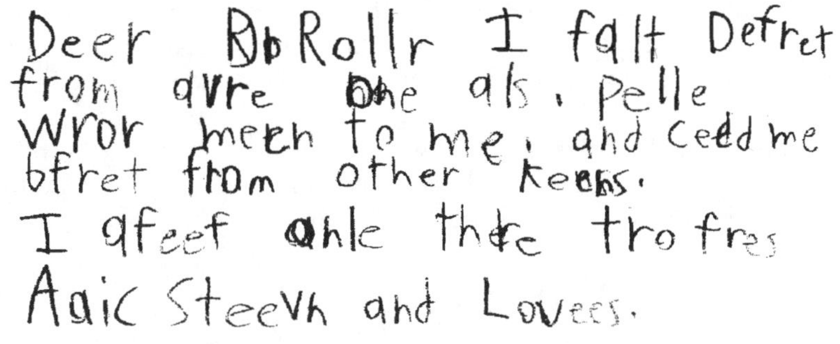
Deer Dr Rollr I falt Defret
from avre ke aks. Pelle
wror meen to me. and ceed me
bfret from other keds.
I afeef ahle there tro fres
Aaic Steevn and Lovees.

Holly's mom wrote this story:

> She [Holly] ran from a friend when she was asked if the book she had was her reading book. She was sobbing by the time she arrived home. I told her we'd ask the teacher if we could cover it.

Karen also hid her reading books at school. She would go the library and get a stack of books—hard ones for the top and bottom and easy ones for the middle—so that no one would see her easy books.

As I reported in Chapter Three there is little evidence that the pull-out programs, remedial programs, or special education programs help children. At worst, some of these programs reduce the instructional time children receive because some regular classroom teachers spend less time with these children, believing that they are not responsible for their reading instruction or development.

On the other hand, some attempts to integrate the children into the regular traditional classroom are frustrating as well. Holly's mom told this story:

> I made a promise to myself that with this move I'd be more passive, and believe it or not within a week I had to go in and discuss why Holly was doing D.O.L. or daily oral language. She'd come home crying and frustrated as to why the other children could complete three D.O.L. sentences and go on to their journals when she couldn't complete one sentence. I could see no purpose to her trying decide which words were misspelled, which didn't make sense, and those that didn't belong when she couldn't even read the sentence. And yet to have her not do them when everyone else is—where do you divide the line? To be different in the class or to be absolutely frustrated. Believe it or not, she wanted both. She's so tired of being different, it even overwhelms me.

Jason's mom wrote the following:

> The one [incident] I'll never forget is when just last year Jason was in fourth grade. Our school was very small and Jason was starting school. [He had moved to a new school for middle school.] It was his first year to be in the regular science class and he was very excited because it was like an honor for him—he had earned the chance to be with other kids he liked to play with. The teacher gave a quiz to the class and made the children correct each other's papers. The paper Jason got to correct, he couldn't read the answers to tell if they were right, and the boy who got Jason's paper held up his hand and told the teacher he couldn't read it and that he got them all wrong. Jason said to me after school all the kids made fun of him and called him stupid. He was so embarrassed and said that he wasn't going back to the class; he didn't care anymore. He said, "What am I trying so hard for to do good, when people just laugh at me and call me stupid?"

To integrate children in classrooms where they cannot succeed is probably as damaging as pulling them out to provide more appropriate instruction. Because many delivery systems for literacy are not working for many children, they need to be changed. Children need instruction that acknowledges variability.

POSSIBILITIES

Because there is little evidence that current organizational programs are working, it might make sense to do what good teachers do in their classrooms—try something else. Variability cannot be denied. We need to accept variability and organize our classrooms to acknowledge and affirm that variability. We need to abandon the archaic notion of grade levels. Workshop classrooms that include children of different ages and abilities are an alternative structure that deserves serious attention.

The workshop structure I use in SRP is well suited to multiage, multiability groupings because it is built around child-centered, choice-based activities. The structures allow everyone to participate: everyone can read something, everyone can write something, everyone can share a book, everyone can share their writing, and everyone can meet with the teacher and other classroom professionals. Yet the structure allows for differentiation. The choice that forms the base of the workshop assumes that everyone will read *different* material and write *different* stories and approach classroom themes in their own way. Choice is a powerful mechanism for accommodating variability.

This is not to say that if we reorganize schools into multiage, multiability groupings and use workshop organizational patterns, *every* child will learn to read. I do think that *most* children would learn to read if this pattern were extended through the entire kindergarten to grade 12 span and if we accepted variability. (However, although I think such an organizational pattern might be adopted at the elementary level, I have no hope that it would be adopted on the secondary level.) If workshops were used in all grade levels, some children would need considerable one-on-one instruction—particularly until readers moved from the emergent to the beginning reading stages when they could read text successfully on their own. Providing enough one-on-one instruction within the school classroom might be difficult.

On the other hand I am loath to pull children out of classrooms for special instruction. In addition to being hard on children, as mentioned, it is hard on teachers. One teacher I know described her classroom as a "train station with [all the] arrivals and departures." I am also reluctant to create separate tutoring stations that only certain children visit within the classroom. It is important that all the children have a sense of equal participation. Pulling children out or aside disturbs their

135

participation and alters their status. Tutoring could be relegated to before- and after-school programs and summer programs. Perhaps this is one of the ways that college and university training programs can be integrated into school structures.

The workshop instructional plan is consistent with all but the second of Walmsley and Allington's (1995, pp. 26–33) principles for reorganizing the delivery of literacy instruction:

1. All staff are responsible for the education of all children.
2. All children are entitled to the same literacy experiences, materials, and expectations.
3. Children should be educated with their peers.
4. We need to define what counts as the literacy curriculum.
5. We need to offer high-quality instruction.
6. We need an organizational infrastructure that supports the teaching of literacy.

The workshop plan would, as the first principle suggests, make all staff responsible for all children's education. Specialists and instructional support personnel would work within classrooms and with all children. Reading specialists might help with reading, and they could help with capable and struggling readers alike. They would be trained to teach each child what skills each child needs. The plan assumes that all children's education will be delivered in the classroom alongside their multiaged, multiability classmates (principle three). What I have suggested as the literacy curriculum—reading and writing workshops—is consistent with what Walmsley and Allington would count as a literacy curriculum (principle four). They argue that at a minimum the literacy curriculum should include reading skills, reading full-length material, reading for a variety of purposes, editing skills, and composing. They also argue that literacy instruction should be integrated with content area subjects and suggest using themes to accomplish the integration. All of this is possible in a workshop classroom.

Principle five, "We need to offer high-quality instruction," is understood. Clearly the type of instructional organization I am proposing requires very knowledgeable and skilled literacy professionals who are trained to collaborate with one another. The infrastructure I have proposed—of specialists and aides working within the classroom and individual tutoring provided in before- and after-school settings and summer settings—would support literacy learning (principle six).

I strongly disagree with principle two—"All children are entitled to the same literacy experiences, materials, and expectations." My disagreement is probably based on a different understanding of what Walmsley and Allington mean by "same" when they apply it to experiences, materials, and expectations. The authors argue that because differentiated instruction has not worked, we should disregard the differential teaching hypothesis:

> If it is true that the major differences between the literacy strategies of better and poorer students can be explained by differences in curriculum, opportunities, and instructional tasks, then there should be no barriers to entitling all children to the same literacy experiences and expectations. (p. 29)

In many classrooms I have observed, I have found all the children reading the same story from the same book. If this is how "same" is interpreted, I am against it. After working with the SRP children and other struggling readers, I do not believe that the major differences between the literacy strategies of better and poor students can be explained fully by differences in curriculum, opportunities, and instructional tasks. I do not believe that the SRP children would have been better off if they had consistently been forced to use materials they could not read. I do not believe that children can learn to read by trying to read books they cannot read. If, on the other hand, "same" means that all the children participate in a reading workshop and choose their own reading materials, I would agree.

Another reason for disagreement may be that we are talking about different children. At SRP, we work primarily with children who are struggling mightily to learn to read. Vellutino (as cited in Tashmar, 1995) and others estimate that only 1 to 3 percent of children in regular school classrooms fall into this group. Walmsley and Allington may be thinking of the much larger group of children, estimates go as high as 20 to 25 percent (Tashmar, 1995), who are labeled as special learners in schools. It may be that many of these children would learn if all children were treated alike. Although we do not know, I do not believe it is true, if treating children alike means having all children read the same materials. Workshop classrooms have the advantage of providing uniform structures in which all children participate, while allowing each child to use materials that are appropriate.

Uniform expectations are also a mistake if they mean that all children should be expected to read at a particular level at a particular age. We have heard a lot about the toll that low expectations exact in children's learning; too high expectations may also exact a costly toll. Karen, a child in SRP, summarized this point well when she turned to me in the middle of a lesson and said the following:

> If I tell you something, I'm not going to hurt your feelings? You see, I don't like to read. Because I can't read very good. And see, I want to read very good. And I can't. So I don't like it much.

What we need are realistic expectations for each child based on the child's actual performance in the classroom. We need skilled teachers who know a lot about literacy development and who can assess children's performance, help them set realistic goals, and help them achieve those goals.

We have always known that there are tremendous individual differences in literacy learning, and yet we persist in offering grade-level, textbook-centered instruction. When the children do not thrive in these environments, we create low reading groups, remedial programs, and pull-out rooms. These special programs and the labels placed on children proliferate, and the children often suffer. It is time we stop trying to "fix" the children and start fixing the schools that often fail them.

Traditional organizational patterns for reading instruction have often trapped caring teachers and children in a system that, despite the quality of the actual instruction, does not help children learn to their full potential. There are alternatives to these patterns. Workshop classrooms allow children to function as equal members of the classroom community, and, at the same time, they allow the children to read materials and write on topics that are appropriate for them. Workshop classrooms are unique in their ability to accommodate the wide range of individual differences in literacy learning and should be used for all children.

References

Allington, R.L. (1977). If they don't read much, how they ever gonna get good? *Journal of Reading, 21,* 57–61.

Allington, R.L. (1983). The reading instruction provided readers of differing abilities. *The Elementary School Journal, 83,* 548–553.

Alvermann, D.E., Dillon, D.R., & O'Brien, D.G. (1987). *Using discussion to promote reading comprehension.* Newark, DE: International Reading Association.

Anderson, R.C., Hiebert, E., Scott, J.A., & Wilkinson, I.A.G. (1985). *Becoming a nation of readers.* Washington, DC: The National Institute of Education.

Anderson, R.C., & Pearson, P.D. (1984). A schema-theoretic view of basic processes in reading comprehension. In P.D. Pearson, R. Barr, M.L. Kamil, & P. Mosenthal (Eds.), *Handbook of reading research* (pp. 255–291). New York: Longman.

Atwell, N. (1987). *In the middle: Writing, reading, and learning with adolescents.* Portsmouth, NH: Heinemann.

Baker, L., & Brown, A.L. (1984). Metacognitive skills in reading. In P.D. Pearson, R. Barr, M.L. Kamil, & P. Mosenthal (Eds.), *Handbook of reading research* (pp. 353–394). New York: Longman.

Barnes, D. (1976). *From communication to curriculum.* Middlesex, England: Penguin.

Beed, P.L., Hawkins, M.E., & Roller, C.M. (1991). Moving learners toward independence: The power of scaffolded instruction. *The Reading Teacher, 44,* 648–655.

Bellack, A., Kleibard, H., Hyman, R., & Smith, F. (1966). *The language of the classroom.* New York: Teachers College Press.

Bruner, J.S. (1975). The ontogenesis of speech acts. *Journal of Child Language, 2,* 1–40.

Calkins, L. (1986). *The art of teaching writing.* Portsmouth, NH: Heinemann.

Cazden, C.B. (1988). *Classroom discourse: The language of teaching and learning.* Portsmouth, NH: Heinemann.

Clay, M.M. (1985). *Early detection of reading difficulties* (3rd ed.). Portsmouth, NH: Heinemann.

Clay, M.M. (1993). *Reading Recovery: A guidebook for teachers in training.* Portsmouth, NH: Heinemann.

Copperman, P. (1986). *Taking books to heart: How to develop a love of reading in your child.* Reading, MA: Addison-Wesley.

Dillon, J.T. (1984). Research on questioning and discussion. *Educational Leadership, 42,* 50–56.

Durkin, D. (1978–79). What classroom observations reveal about reading comprehension instruction. *Reading Research Quarterly, 14,* 481–533.

Edelsky, C., Altwerger, B., & Flores, B. (1991). *Whole language: What's the difference?* Portsmouth, NH: Heinemann.

Fielding, L.F., & Roller, C.M. (1992). Making difficult books accessible and easy books acceptable. *The Reading Teacher, 45*, 678–685.

Finders, M.J. (1994). *Just girls: A study of the uses of literacy by early adolescent girls.* Unpublished dissertation, University of Iowa, Iowa City.

Forbes, R., & Roller, C.M. (1991). The relationship of instructional level placement and the informal reading inventory to the process instruction of reading. *Iowa Reading Journal, 4(2)*, 3–9.

Ford, M.P., & Ohlhausen, M.M. (1988). Tips from reading clinics for coping with disabled readers in regular classrooms. *The Reading Teacher, 42*, 18–22.

Forsyth, S. (1993, December 4). *The validity and reliability of literacy portfolios in differentiating levels of students' reading performance.* Paper presented at The National Reading Conference, Charleston, SC.

Gonzalez, N.L. (1994, December 4). *Nancy Drew: Girls' literature, women's reading groups, and the transmission of literacy.* Paper presented at the National Reading Conference, San Diego, CA.

Goodman, K. (1986). *What's whole in whole language?* Portsmouth, NH: Heinemann.

Gough, P.B. (1972). One second of reading. In J.F. Kavanogh & I.G. Mattingly (Eds.), *Language by car and by eye* (pp. 331–358). Cambridge, MA: MIT Press.

Graves, D. (1983). *Writing: Teachers and children at work.* Portsmouth, NH: Heinemann.

Hansen, J. (1987). *When writers read.* Portsmouth, NH: Heinemann.

Herman, P.A. (1985). The effect of repeated readings on reading rate, speech pauses, and word recognition accuracy. *Reading Research Quarterly, 20*, 553–565.

Hoetker, J., & Ahlbrand, W.P. (1969). The persistence of recitation. *American Education Research Journal, 6*, 145–166.

Hornsby, D., Sukarna, D., & Parry, J. (1986a). *Read on: A conference approach to reading.* Portsmouth, NH: Heinemann.

Hornsby, D., Sukarna, D., & Parry, J. (1986b). *Write on: A conference approach to writing.* Portsmouth, NH: Heinemann.

Hunt, L. (1970). The effect of self selection, interest, and motivation upon independent, instructional and frustration levels. *The Reading Teacher, 24*, 146–151.

Hunter, M.C. (1976). Improved instruction. El Segundo, CA: TIP Publications.

Labbo, L., & Teale, W.H. (1990). Cross-age reading: A strategy for helping poor readers. *The Reading Teacher, 43*, 362–369.

Lewis, C. (1995). *The social drama of literature discussions in a fifth/sixth grade classroom.* Unpublished dissertation, University of Iowa, Iowa City.

Malone, T.W., & Lepper, M.R. (1987). Making learning fun; A taxonomy of intrinsic motivations for learning. In R.E. Snow & M.J. Farr (Eds.), *Aptitude, learning, and instruction, Vol 3: Cognitive and affective process analyses* (pp. 223–253). Hillsdale, NJ: Erlbaum.

Marshall, J.D., Smagorinsky, P., & Smith, M.W. (1995). *The language of interpretation: Patterns of discourse in discussions of literature.* Urbana, IL: National Council of Teachers of English.

Mehan, H. (1979). *Learning lessons.* Cambridge, MA: Harvard University Press.

National Center for Education Statistics. (1995). *1994 NAEP reading: A first look—Findings from the National Assessment of Educational Progress.* Washington, DC: US Government Printing Office.

National Commission on Excellence in Education. (1983). *A nation at risk: The imperative for educational reform.* Washington, DC: US Government Printing Office.

Ohlhausen, M.M., & Jepsen, M. (1992). Lessons from Goldilocks: Somebody's been choosing my books but I can make my own choices now. *The New Advocate, 5*(1), 31–46.

Pearson, P.D., & Gallagher, M.C. (1983). The instruction of reading comprehension. *Contemporary Educational Psychology, 8*, 317–344.

Phillips, G., & McNaughton, S. (1990). The practice of storybook reading to preschool children in mainstream New Zealand families. *Reading Research Quarterly, 25*, 196–212.

Roller, C.M. (1989). Classroom interaction patterns: Reflections of a stratified society. *Language Arts, 66*, 492–500.

Roller, C.M., & Beed, P.L. (1994). Sometimes the conversations were grand, and sometimes... *Language Arts, 71*, 509–515.

Rumelhart, D.E. (1977). Toward an interactive model of reading. In S. Dornic (Ed.), *Attention and performance VI*. Hillsdale, NJ: Erlbaum.

Samuels, S.J. (1979). The method of repeated readings. *The Reading Teacher, 32*, 403–408.

Smith, F. (1971). *Understanding reading*. New York: Rinehart & Winston.

Stanovich, K.E. (1986). Matthew effects in reading: Some consequences of individual differences in the acquisition of literacy. *Reading Research Quarterly, 21*, 360–407.

Tashmar, B. (1995). Misreading dyslexia. *Scientific American*, 14–16.

Teale, W.H. (1990). The promise and challenge of informal assessment in early literacy. In L. Morrow & J. Smith (Eds.), *Assessment in early literacy*. Englewood Cliffs, NJ: Prentice Hall.

Tough, J. (1985). *Talking and learning*. London: School Curriculum Development Committee.

Vellutino, F.R. (1987). Dyslexia. *Scientific American, 256*(3), 34–41.

Vygotsky, L. (1978). *Mind in society*. Cambridge, MA: Harvard University Press.

Walmsley, S.A., & Allington, R.L. (1995). Redefining and reforming instructional support programs for at-risk students. In R.L. Allington & S.A. Walmsley (Eds.), *No quick fix: Rethinking literacy programs in America's elementary schools*. New York: Teachers College Press, and Newark, DE: International Reading Association.

Wasik, B., & Slavin, R. (1993). Preventing early reading failure with one-to-one tutoring. A review of five programs. *Reading Research Quarterly, 28*, 179–200.

Wells, G. (1986). *The meaning makers: Children learning language and using language to learn*. Portsmouth, NH: Heinemann.

Wood, D., Bruner, J., & Ross, G. (1976). The role of tutoring in problem solving. *Journal of Child Psychology and Psychiatry, 17*, 89–100.

Wood, D., Wood, H., & Middleton, D. (1978). An experimental evaluation of four face-to-face teaching strategies. *International Journal of Behavioral Development, 1*, 131–147.

Literature Cited

Ackerman, K. (1988). *Song and dance man*. Illustrated by S. Gammell. New York: Knopf.

Adams, P., Hartson, E., & Taylor, M. (1982). *Hi dog!* Illustrated by D. Hockerman. Chicago, IL: Follett.

Allen, P. (1983). *Who sank the boat*. New York: Coward-McCann.

Arnosky, J. (1986). *Deer at the brook*. New York: Lothrop, Lee & Shepard.

Bang, M. (1985). *The paper crane*. New York: Greenwillow.

Berenstain, S., & Berenstain, J. (1964). *The bike lesson*. New York: Random House.

Berenstain, S., & Berenstain, J. (1978). *The spooky old tree*. New York: Random House.

Charlip, R. (1980). *Fortunately*. New York: Four Winds.

Cole, J. (1989). *Anna Banana: 101 jump rope rhymes*. New York: Morrow.

Cole, J. (1991). *My puppy is born*. New York: Morrow.

Cole, J., & Calmenson, S. (1990). *Miss Mary Mack and other children's street rhymes*. New York: Morrow.

Cowley, J. (1980). *Mrs. Wishy Washy*. San Diego, CA: The Wright Group.

Cowley, J. (1981). *The bee*. Illustrated by C. Ross. San Diego, CA: The Wright Group.

Cowley, J. (1981). *Round and round*. Illustrated by D. Cowe. San Diego, CA: The Wright Group.

Cowley, J. (1982). *Danger!* Illustrated by D. Gardiner. San Diego, CA: The Wright Group.

Cowley, J. (1982). *Horace*. Illustrated by A. Dickeson. San Diego, CA: The Wright Group.

Cowley, J. (1983). *If you meet a dragon*. Illustrated by R. Parkinson. San Diego, CA: The Wright Group.

Cowley, J. (1986). *Our street*. Illustrated by M. Beasley. San Diego, CA: The Wright Group.

Cowley, J., & Melser, J. (1980). *In a dark, dark wood*. San Diego, CA: The Wright Group.

Dangarembga, T. (1988). *Nervous conditions*. London: Women's Press.

Dolch, E.W., & Dolch, M.P. (1959). *Dog pals*. Illustrated by F. Mafera. Champaign, IL: Garrard.

Drew, D. (1987). *Tadpole diary*. London: Rigby.

Fox, M. (1990). *Guess what?* Illustrated by V. Goodman. New York: Harcourt, Brace, Jovanovich.

Giff, P.R. (1984). *The beast in Ms. Rooney's room*. Illustrated by B. Sims. New York: Dell.

Giff, P.R. (1984). *The candy corn contest*. Illustrated by B. Sims. New York: Dell.

Giff, P.R. (1988). *Donald Morgan goes to bat*. Illustrated by S. Natti. New York: Viking Penguin.

Harris, S. (1979). *Boats and ships*. New York: Franklin Watts.

Hayes, S. (1986). *This is the bear*. Illustrated by H. Craig. New York: Lippincott.

Heath, D.C. (1989). *Turtles like to sleep in*. Illustrated by B. Dodson. New York: D.C. Heath.

Kessler, L. (1965). *Here comes the strikeout*. New York: HarperCollins.

Koblenz, J. (1984). *Corvette: America's Sports Car*. New York: Beekman House.

Lobel, A. (1979). *Days with frog and toad*. New York: HarperCollins.

Martin, B.M., Jr. (1983). *Brown bear, brown bear, what do you see?* Illustrated by E. Carle. New York: Holt, Rinehart, Winston.

Martin, B.M., Jr. (1991). *Polar bear, polar bear, what do you see?* New York: Holt, Rinehart, Winston.

McWhirter, N. (1988). *Guinness book of world records*. New York: Bantam.

Melser, J. (1980). *Lazy Mary*. San Diego, CA: The Wright Group.

Melser, J. (1981). *Fiddle-dee-dee*. San Diego, CA: The Wright Group.

Munsch, R. (1985). *Thomas' snowsuit*. Illustrated by M. Marchenko. Toronto, Canada: Annick Press.

National Wildlife Federation. *Ranger Rick*. Vienna, VA: Author.

Numeroff, L.J. (1985). *If you give a moose a cookie*. Illustrated by F. Bond. New York: HarperCollins.

Numeroff, L.J. (1991). *If you give a moose a muffin*. Illustrated by F. Bond. New York: HarperCollins.

Otto, C.B. (1990). *That sky, that rain*. Illustrated by M. Lloyd. New York: Harper Trophy.

Raabe, J.A. (1975). *Dune bug*. Illustrated by E. Ian. Cleveland, OH: Modern Curriculum.

Raffi. (1987). *Shake my sillies out*. Illustrated by D. Allender. New York: Crown.

Resciniti, A.G. (1983). *Baseball's heavy hitters*. Pinellas Park, FL: Willowisp Press.

Rigby Education. (1985). *The bulldozer cleared the way*. Crystal Lake, IL: Author.

Schick, E. (1969). *City in the summer*. New York: Macmillan.

Scott Foresman Reading Systems. (1971). *Cats and kittens*. Glenview, IL: Scott, Foresman.

Shaw, N. (1986). *Sheep in a jeep*. Illustrated by M. Apple. New York: Houghton Mifflin.

Steig, W. (1982). *Doctor DeSoto*. New York: Farrar, Strauss and Giroux.

Van Allsburg, C. (1987). *The Z was zapped: A play in twenty-six acts*. Boston, MA: Houghton Mifflin.

West, C. (1986). *Have you seen the crocodile?* New York: HarperCollins.

West, C. (1986). *"Pardon," said the giraffe*. New York: HarperCollins.

Wood, A. (1985). *King Bidgood's in the bathtub*. Illustrated by D. Wood. New York: Harcourt, Brace, Jovanovich.

Resources

by Paula O. Brandt

RESOURCES FOR IDENTIFYING CHILDREN'S BOOKS FOR STRUGGLING READERS

The following resources include reading and interest levels.

Barstow, Barbara, and Judith Riggle. *Beyond Picture Books: A Guide to First Readers*. (2nd ed.). Bowker, 1995.

> This title is a little misleading because nearly all the books cited in this source would be shelved with picture books in libraries. A list of several hundred "outstanding first readers" opens this book and is followed by an annotated bibliography of almost 2,500 books that is arranged alphabetically by author. The subject, readability, and series indexes are very useful.

Fleming, Carolyn Sherwood, and Donna Schatt, Editors. *Choices: A Core Collection for Young Reluctant Readers*. John Gordon Burke, 1983.

> *Choices* is an oddly arranged listing of 360 titles. The first section is arranged by author, and the second section is arranged by subject. Included alphabetically as subjects are "Interest Level" (K–2 through 6+) and "Reading Level" (1.1 through 5.1). All entries, in both sections, feature lengthy annotations.

Lee, Lauren K., Editor. *The Elementary School Library Collection: A Guide to Books and Other Media*. Brodart, 1994.

> In this standard reference source that helps prioritize materials purchased by libraries, each of the books is assigned an interest level and a reading level. The annotated titles are arranged in the order they would typically be found on a library shelf—in the "easy," "fiction," or "dewey" sections. There's a subject index and several helpful appendices, including "Books for Independent Reading" arranged by reading level, "Author's Series," and "Publisher's Series."

Pilla, Marianne Laino. *The Best: High/Low Books for Reluctant Readers*. Libraries Unlimited, 1990.

> Arranged alphabetically by author, these books are for reluctant readers in grades 3 to 12 who are reading two or more levels below their grade level. Each entry includes the interest level and the reading level, using Fry, and a brief annotation. This source has subject, grade-level, and reading-level indexes.

Pilla, Marianne Laino. *Resources for Middle-Grade Reluctant Readers*. Libraries Unlimited, 1987.

> One of the six chapters in this book is an annotated bibliography, by subject, of children's books. Interest levels and reading levels are also included. The other chapters offer information about how to identify and work with reluctant readers and how to evaluate and select books for them.

Wilson, George, and Joyce Moss. *Books for Children to Read Alone: A Guide for Parents and Librarians, Pre-K Through Grade 3*. Bowker, 1988.

> This is an easy-to-use listing arranged by grade level. Preceding the annotations for each level, the authors and titles are listed that are "easy," "average," and "challenging." Series, subject, and readability indexes increase the usefulness of this book.

OTHER SOURCES OF RECOMMENDED BOOKS

Children's Books of the Year. Child Study Children's Book Committee. Annual.

> This "best" list includes a short annotated list of beginning readers.

"Easy Reading" column, appears quarterly in *Booklist*, a reviewing source published bimonthly by the American Library Association.

Gillespie, John T. *Best Books for Children: Preschool Through Grade 6*. (5th ed.). Bowker, 1994.

> Following over 4,000 picture book annotations is a section of annotations for beginning readers in this resource.

Horn Book Guide to Children's and Young Adult Books, published biannually by Horn Book, Inc.

This publication briefly reviews, among other books, recently published picture books, easy readers, and younger fiction. It includes a subject index and a series index.

Jensen, Julie M., and Nancy L. Roser, Editors. *Adventuring with Books: A Booklist for Pre-K–Grade 6.* (10th ed.). National Council of Teachers of English, 1993.

Although this book is arranged differently with each edition, this particular edition includes a small list of annotated recommended easy-reading books in the chapter on language and reading.

Lima, Carolyn W., and John A. Lima. *A to Zoo: Subject Access to Children's Picture Books.* (4th ed.). Bowker, 1994.

This is the best source for identifying picture books on a broad range of subjects. The subject "Cumulative Tales" is especially useful when searching for repetitive stories.

Lipson, Eden Ross. *The New York Times Parent's Guide to the Best Books for Children.* Random House, 1991.

An entire chapter of this source is devoted to early reading books.

More Kids' Favorite Books: A Compilation of Children's Choices 1992–1994. Children's Book Council and the International Reading Association, 1995.

Two chapters, "Beginning Independent Reading" and "Younger Readers," offer annotated bibliographies of recent titles that have been popular with children.

SUGGESTED TITLES, SERIES, AND AUTHORS

Books with Repetitive Phrases

Accorsi, William. *Billy's Button.* Greenwillow, 1992.
Allen, Pamela. *Fancy That.* Orchard, 1988.
Allen, Pamela. *I Wish I Had a Pirate Suit.* Viking, 1990.
Allen, Pamela. *Who Sank the Boat?* Putnam, 1990.
Anholt, Catherine. *Good Days, Bad Days.* Putnam, 1991.
Archambault, John, and Bill Martin, Jr. *The Beautiful Feast for a Big King Cat.* Ill. Bruce Degen. HarperCollins, 1994.
Aylesworth, Jim. *Mr. Mcgill Goes to Town.* Ill. Thomas Graham. Holt, 1989.

Aylesworth, Jim. *My Son John*. Ill. David Frampton. Holt, 1994.

Aylesworth, Jim. *Old Black Fly*. Ill. Stephen Gammell. Holt, 1992.

Baer, Gene. *Thump, Thump, Rat-a-Tat-Tat*. HarperCollins, 1989.

Baker, Keith. *Who Is the Beast?* Harcourt, 1990.

Bourgeois, Paulette. *Too Many Chickens*. Ill. Bill Slavin. Little, 1991.

Brisson, Pat. *Benny's Pennies*. Ill. Bob Barner. Doubleday, 1993.

Brown, Craig. *In the Spring*. Greenwillow, 1994.

Brown, Craig. *My Barn*. Greenwillow, 1991.

Burningham, John. *Hey! Get off Our Train*. Crown, 1990.

Carle, Eric. *Draw Me a Star*. Putnam, 1992.

Carle, Eric. *The Mixed-Up Chameleon*. HarperCollins, 1988.

Carle, Eric. *Today Is Monday*. Putnam, 1993.

Carle, Eric. *The Very Busy Spider*. Putnam, 1989.

Carle, Eric. *The Very Hungry Caterpillar*. Putnam, 1981.

Carle, Eric. *The Very Quiet Cricket*. Putnam, 1990.

Carlstrom, Nancy White. *What Would You Do If You Lived at the Zoo?* Ill. Lizi Boyd. Little, 1994.

Carlstrom, Nancy White. *Who Gets the Sun out of Bed?* Ill. David McPhail. Little, 1992.

Carter, David. *In a Dark, Dark Wood*. Simon & Schuster, 1991.

Cazet, Denys. *Nothing at All*. Orchard, 1994.

Charlip, Remy. *Fortunately*. Macmillan, 1984.

Christelow, Eileen. *Five Little Monkeys Jumping on the Bed*. Houghton, 1989.

Christelow, Eileen. *Five Little Monkeys Sitting in a Tree*. Clarion, 1991.

Cowen-Fletcher, Jane. *It Takes a Village*. Scholastic, 1994.

Coxe, Molly. *Whose Footprints?* HarperCollins, 1990.

Cuyler, Margery. *That's Good, That's Bad*. Ill. David Catrow. Holt, 1991.

De Regniers, Beatrice. *How Joe the Bear and Sam the Mouse Got Together*. Ill. Bernice Myers. Lothrop, 1990.

DeZutter, Hank. *Who Says a Dog Goes Bow-Wow?* Ill. Suse Macdonald. Doubleday, 1993.

Dodds, Dayle Ann. *The Color Box*. Ill. Giles Laroche. Little, 1992.

Dodds, Dayle Ann. *Wheel Away*. Ill. Thacher Hurd. HarperCollins, 1989.

Duffy, Deborah. *Barnyard Tracks*. Ill. Janet P. Marshall. Boyds Mills, 1992.

Duke, Kate. *If You Walk Down This Road*. Dutton, 1993.

Dunbar, Joyce. *Four Fierce Kittens*. Ill. Jakki Wood. Scholastic, 1992.

Ericsson, Jennifer. *No Milk!* Ill. Ora Eitan. Morrow, 1993.

Evans, Katie. *Hunky Dory Ate It*. Ill. Janet M. Stocke. Dutton, 1992.

Evans, Katie. *Hunky Dory Found It*. Ill. Janet M. Stocke. Dutton, 1994.

Fleming, Denise. *Barnyard Banter*. Holt, 1994.

Fleming, Denise. *In the Small, Small Pond*. Holt, 1993.

Fleming, Denise. *In the Tall, Tall Grass*. Holt, 1991.

Fleming, Denise. *Lunch*. Holt, 1992.

Fox, Mem. *Hattie and the Fox*. Ill. Patricia Mullins. Macmillan, 1988.

Fox, Mem. *Night Noises*. Ill. Terry Denton. Harcourt, 1989.

Fox, Mem. *Shoes from Grandpa*. Ill. Patricia Mullins. Orchard, 1990.

Fox, Mem. *Time for Bed*. Ill. Jane Dyer. Harcourt, 1993.

Gelman, Rita. *I Went to the Zoo*. Ill. Maryann Kovalski. Scholastic, 1993.

Gilman, Phoebe. *Something from Nothing*. Scholastic, 1993.

Gomi, Taro. *My Friends*. Chronicle, 1990.

Goode, Diane. *Where's Our Mama?* Dutton, 1991.

Griffith, Helen. *Plunk's Dreams.* Greenwillow, 1990.

Gross, Theodore. *Everyone Asked About You.* Ill. Sheila Samton. Putnam, 1990.

Guarino, Deborah. *Is Your Mama a Llama?* Ill. Steven Kellogg. Scholastic, 1989.

Guy, Ginger Foglesong. *Black Crow, Black Crow.* Ill. Nancy Winslow Parker. Greenwillow, 1991.

Gwynne, Fred. *Easy to See Why.* Simon & Schuster, 1993.

Hadithi, Mwenye. *Lazy Lion.* Ill. Adrienne Kennaway. Little, 1990.

Hamm, Diane. *Rockabye Farm.* Ill. Richard Brown. Simon & Schuster, 1992.

Hellen, Nancy. *The Bus Stop.* Orchard, 1988.

Hennessy, B.G. *Jake Baked the Cake.* Ill. Mary Morgan. Viking, 1990.

Hersom, Kathleen. *The Copycat.* Ill. Catherine Stock. Atheneum, 1989.

Hutchins, Pat. *The Doorbell Rang.* Greenwillow, 1986.

Hutchins, Pat. *Little Pink Pig.* Greenwillow, 1994.

Hutchins, Pat. *Silly Billy.* Greenwillow, 1992.

Hutchins, Pat. *What Game Shall We Play?* Greenwillow, 1990.

Kalan, Robert. *Stop, Thief!* Ill. Yossi Abolafia. Greenwillow, 1993.

Kasza, Keiko. *The Pig's Picnic.* Putnam, 1988.

Kasza, Keiko. *When the Elephant Walks.* Putnam, 1990.

Kasza, Keiko. *The Wolf's Chicken Stew.* Putnam, 1987.

Kimmel, Eric. *I Took My Frog to the Library.* Ill. Blanche Sims. Viking, 1990.

Komaiko, Leah. *My Perfect Neighborhood.* Ill. Barbara Westman. HarperCollins, 1990.

Lacome, Julie. *Walking Through the Jungle.* Candlewick, 1993.

Levinson, Riki. *I Go with My Family to Grandma's.* Ill. Diane Goode. Dutton, 1986.

Lewison, Cheyette. *Going to Sleep on the Farm.* Ill. Juan Wijngaard. Dial, 1992.

Lillegard, Dee. *Sitting in My Box.* Ill. Jon Agee. Dutton, 1989.

Lindbergh, Reeve. *The Day the Goose Got Loose.* Ill. Steven Kellogg. Dial, 1990.

Lindbergh, Reeve. *There's a Cow in the Road.* Ill. Tracey Campbell Pearson. Dial, 1993.

London, Jonathan. *Froggy Gets Dressed.* Ill. Frank Remkiewicz. Viking, 1992.

Lyon, George Ella. *The Outside Inn.* Ill. Vera Rosenberry. Orchard, 1991.

MacDonald, E. *Mr. Macgregor's Breakfast Egg.* Ill. Ayliffe Alex. Viking, 1990.

Maris, Ron. *Are You There, Bear?* Greenwillow, 1985.

Maris, Ron. *Bernard's Boring Day.* Delacorte, 1990.

Martin, Bill. *Brown Bear, Brown Bear, What Do You See?* Ill. Eric Carle. Holt, 1983.

Martin, Bill. *Chicka Chicka Boom Boom.* Ill. Lois Ehlert. Simon & Schuster, 1993.

Martin, Bill. *The Happy Hippopotami.* Ill. Betsy Everitt. Harcourt, 1991.

Martin, Bill. *Here Are My Hands.* Ill. Ted Rand. Holt, 1987.

Martin, Bill. *The Maestro Plays.* Ill. Sal Murdocca. Holt, 1970.

Martin, Bill. *Old Devil Wind.* Ill. Barry Root. Harcourt, 1993.

Martin, Bill. *Polar Bear, Polar Bear, What Do You Hear?* Ill. Eric Carle. Holt, 1991.

McDonald, Megan. *Is This a House for Hermit Crab?* Ill. S. D. Schindler. Orchard, 1990.

McGuire, Richard. *Night Becomes Day.* Viking, 1994.

McNally, Darcie, Adapt. *In a Cabin in a Wood.* Ill. Robin Michal Koontz. Cobblehill, 1991.

Melmed, Laura. *The First Song Ever Sung.* Ill. Ed Young. Lothrop, 1993.

Neitzel, Shirley. *The Bag I'm Taking to Grandma's.* Ill. Nancy Winslow Parker. Greenwillow, 1995.

Neitzel, Shirley. *The Dress I'll Wear to the Party.* Ill. Nancy Winslow Parker. Greenwillow, 1992.

Neitzel, Shirley. *The Jacket I Wear in the Snow.* Greenwillow, 1989.

Noll, Sally. *Lucky Morning*. Greenwillow, 1994.

Numeroff, Laura. *If You Give a Moose a Muffin*. Ill. Felicia Bond. HarperCollins, 1991.

Numeroff, Laura. *If You Give a Mouse a Cookie*. Ill. Felicia Bond. HarperCollins, 1985.

Paxton, Tom. *Where's the Baby?* Ill. Mark Graham. Morrow, 1993.

Pomerantz, Charlotte. *Here Comes Henny*. Ill. Nancy Winslow Parker. Greenwillow, 1994.

Pomerantz, Charlotte. *Where's the Bear?* Ill. Byron Barton. Greenwillow, 1994.

Reiser, Lynn. *Any Kind of Dog*. Ill. Amy Cohn. Morrow, 1994.

Rose, Agatha. *Hide and Seek in the Yellow House*. Ill. Kate Spohn. Viking, 1992.

Rosen, Michael. *We're Going on a Bear Hunt*. Ill. Helen Oxenbury. Macmillan, 1989.

Rounds, Glen. *I Know an Old Lady Who Swallowed a Fly*. Holiday, 1990.

Sage, Angie. *The Trouble with Babies*. Ill. Chris Sage. Viking, 1989.

Schertle, Alice. *Little Frog's Song*. Ill. Leonard Everett Fisher. HarperCollins, 1992.

Schertle, Alice. *That's What I Thought*. Ill. John Wallner. Harper, 1990.

Scott, Ann Herbert. *Hi*. Ill. Glo Coalson. Putnam, 1994.

Serfozo, Mary. *Who Said Red?* Ill. Keiko Narahaski. Macmillan, 1992.

Serfozo, Mary. *Who Wants One?* Ill. Keiko Narahashi. Macmillan, 1989.

Silverman, Erica. *Big Pumpkin*. Ill. S. D. Schindler. Macmillan, 1992.

Stutson, Caroline. *By the Light of the Halloween Moon*. Ill. Kevin Hawkes. Puffin, 1994.

Sweet, Melissa. *Fiddle-I-Fee*. Little, 1992.

Tafuri, Nancy. *Have You Seen My Duckling?* Viking, 1986.

Townson, Hazel. *Terrible Tuesday*. Ill. Tony Ross. Morrow, 1985.

Van Laan, Nancy. *The Big Fat Worm*. Ill. Marisabina Russo. Knopf, 1987.

Van Laan, Nancy. *A Mouse in My House*. Ill. Marjorie Priceman. Knopf, 1990.

Van Laan, Nancy. *People, People Everywhere*. Ill. Nadine Bernard Westcott. Knopf, 1992.

Van Laan, Nancy. *Possum Come-a-Knockin'*. Ill. George Booth. Knopf, 1990.

Van Laan, Nancy. *This Is the Hat*. Ill. Holly Mead. Little, 1992.

Van Laan, Nancy. *The Tiny, Tiny Boy and the Big, Big Cow*. Ill. Marjorie Priceman. Knopf, 1993.

Waddell, Martin. *Can't You Sleep, Little Bear?* Ill. Barbara Firth. Candlewick, 1992.

Waddell, Martin. *Farmer Duck*. Ill. Helen Oxenbury. Candlewick, 1992.

Waddell, Martin. *Sailor Bear*. Ill. Virginia Austin. Candlewick, 1992.

Walton, Sherry. *Books Are for Eating*. Ill. Sherry Walton. Dutton, 1990.

Weiss, Nicki. *Dog Boy Cap Skate*. Greenwillow, 1989.

Weiss, Nicki. *An Egg Is an Egg*. Putnam, 1990.

Weiss, Nicki. *On a Hot, Hot Day*. Putnam, 1992.

Weiss, Nicki. *Sun Sand Sea Sail*. Greenwillow, 1989.

Weiss, Nicki. *Where Does the Brown Bear Go?* Puffin, 1989.

Wellington, Monica. *The Sheep Follow*. Dutton, 1992.

Wickstrom, Sylvie. *Turkey on the Loose*. Dial, 1990.

Williams, Linda. *The Little Old Lady Who Was Not Afraid of Anything*. Ill. Megan Lloyd. HarperCollins, 1986.

Williams, Sue. *I Went Walking*. Ill. Julie Vivas. Harcourt, 1990.

Williams, Suzanne. *Mommy Doesn't Know My Name*. Ill. Andrew Shachat. Houghton, 1990.

Wilson, Etta. *Music in the Night*. Ill. Robin M. Koontz. Dutton, 1993.

Wood, Audrey. *King Bidgood's in the Bathtub*. Ill. Don Wood. Harcourt, 1985.

Wood, Audrey. *The Napping House*. Ill. Don Wood. Harcourt, 1984.

Wood, Audrey. *Silly Sally*. Harcourt, 1992.

Beginning-to-Read Series and Collections

Bank Street Ready-to-Read Series (Levels 1, 2, 3). Bantam
Chicago and the Cat Series by Robin M. Koontz. Dutton
Cole, Joanna, and Stephanie Calmenson, Compilers. *Ready...Set...Read! The Beginning Reader's Treasury.* Doubleday.
Dial Easy-to-Read Series. Dial
Dragon Tales Series by Dav Pilkey. Orchard
Eyewitness Junior Series. Knopf
Hello Reader Series (Levels 1, 2, 3, 4). Scholastic
Hello Reading Series by Harriet Ziefert. Viking/Puffin
Henry and Mudge Series by Cynthia Rylant. Macmillan
I Can Read Series. HarperCollins
Let's-Read-and-Find-Out Science Series (Stages 1, 2). HarperCollins
Mr. Putter and Tabby Series by Cynthia Rylant. Harcourt Brace
Pinky and Rex Series by James Howe. Macmillan
The Random House Book of Easy-to-Read Stories. Random House
Ronald Morgan Series by Patricia Reilly Giff. Viking/Puffin
Step into Reading Series (Steps 1, 2, 3, 4). Random House
Step into Science Series. Random House

Chapter Books Series and Collections

Adam Joshua Series by Janice Lee Smith. HarperCollins
Amber Brown Series by Paula Danziger. Putnam
Best Enemy Series by Kathleen Leverich. Greenwillow
Cam Jansen Series by David A. Adler. Viking
A First Stepping Stone Book Series. Random House
Horrible Harry, Song Lee, and Mary Marony Series by Suzy Kline. Viking
I Hate Series, and Other Titles, by P. J. Petersen. Dutton
Meg Mackintosh Series by Lucinda Landon. Little Brown
New Kids at the Polk Street School Series by Patricia Reilly Giff. Dell Young Yearling
Rats on the Roof and *Rats on the Range* by James Marshall. Dial
Redfeather Series. Henry Holt
Springboard Books Series. Little Brown
Stepping Stone Series. Random House

Chapter Books, Nonseries

Byars, Betsy. *Beans on the Roof.* Delacorte, 1988.
Caseley, Judith. *Harry and Arney.* Greenwillow, 1994.
Demuth, Patricia Brennan. *In Trouble with Teacher.* Dutton, 1995.
Hest, Amy. *Nannies for Hire.* Morrow, 1994.
Hooks, William H. *The Girl Who Could Fly.* Simon & Schuster, 1995.

Kroll, Steven. *I'm George Washington and You're Not.* Hyperion, 1994.
Myers, Laurie. *Guinea Pigs Don't Talk.* Houghton Mifflin, 1994.
Petersen, P. J. *The Amazing Magic Show.* Simon & Schuster, 1994.
Wittman, Sally. *Stepbrother Sabotage.* HarperCollins, 1994.
Wojciechowski, Susan. *Don't Call Me Beanhead.* Candlewick, 1994.

Authors of Easy-to-Read Informational Books

Some of these authors also write more difficult books.

Aliki
Arnold, Caroline
Adler, David. Picture Book Biography Series
Barton, Byron
Branley, Franklyn
Cole, Joanna. The Magic School Bus Series, and others
Florian, Douglas. How We Work Series, and others
Hirschi, Ron
Gibbons, Gail
Lauber, Patricia
Lavies, Bianca
Leedy, Loreen
Markle, Susan
McMillan, Bruce
Morris, Ann
Rockwell, Anne
Showers, Paul

Author Index

Note: An "f" following an index entry indicates that the citation may be found in a figure.

W

Walmsley, S.A., 8, 9, 29, 136–137
Wasik, B., 82
Wells, G., 30, 31, 33, 35, 44
West, C., 57–58, 59–61
Wilkinson, I.A.G., 29
Wood, A., 5, 50
Wood, D., 75
Wood, H., 75

Subject Index

Note: An "f" following an index entry indicates that the citation may be found in a figure.

R